17

H E I N E M A N N

S H A K E S P E A R E

Twelfth Night
or
What You Will

edited by Andrew Worrall

with additional notes and activities by
Rick Lee, Rob Chambers, Victor Juszkiewicz
and Llinos Davies

Series Editor: John Seely

*In association with the RSA
Shakespeare in Schools Project*

The RSA Shakespeare in Schools Project

The **Heinemann Shakespeare Series** has been developed in association with the **RSA Shakespeare in Schools Project**. Schools in the project have trialled teaching approaches to make Shakespeare accessible to students of all ages and ability levels.

John Seely has worked with schools in the project to develop the unique way of teaching Shakespeare to 11- to 16-year-olds found in **Heinemann Shakespeares**.

The project is a partnership between the RSA (Royal Society for the encouragement of Arts, Manufactures and Commerce), Leicestershire County Council and the Groby family of schools in Leicestershire. It is co-ordinated by the Knighton Fields Advisory Centre for Drama and Dance.

Heinemann Educational Publishers
Halley Court, Jordan Hill, Oxford OX2 8EJ
a division of Reed Educational & Professional Publishing Ltd
OXFORD   MELBOURNE   AUCKLAND
JOHANNESBURG   BLANTYRE   GABORONE
IBADAN   PORTSMOUTH (NH) USA   CHICAGO

Introduction, notes and activities © Andrew Worrall, John Seely, Rick Lee 1994
Additional material by Rob Chambers, Victor Juszkiewicz and Llinos Davies

The text is based on the First Folio, with the addition of some stage directions to make the action more comprehensible.

Printed in the *Heinemann Shakespeare Plays* series 1994

03 02 01
12 11

A catalogue record for this book is available from the British Library on request.
ISBN 0 435 19204 3

Cover design Miller Craig and Cocking
Cover photograph from Donald Cooper

Produced by Green Door Design Ltd

Printed by Clays Ltd, St Ives plc

Contents

Introduction: using this book

This is more than just an edition of *Twelfth Night* with a few notes. It is a complete guide to studying and enjoying the play.

It begins with an introduction to Shakespeare's theatre, and to the story and characters of the play.

At the end of the book there is guidance on studying the play:

- how to keep track of things as you work
- how to take part in a range of drama activities
- understanding Shakespeare's language
- exploring the main themes of the play
- studying the characters
- how to write about the play.

There are also questions and a glossary of specialist words you need when working on the play.

The central part of the book is, of course, the play itself. Here there are several different kinds of help on offer:

Summary: at the top of each double page there is a short summary of what happens on that page.

Grading: alongside the text is a shaded band to help you when working on the play:

1 This is very important text that you probably need to spend extra time on.

2 This is text that you need to read carefully.

3 This is text that you need to spend less time on.

Notes: difficult words, phrases and sentences are explained in simple English.

Extra summaries: for the 'white' text the notes are replaced by numbered summaries that give more detail than the ordinary page-by-page summaries.

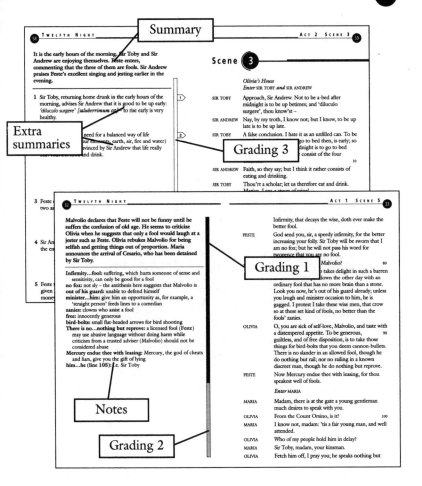

Summary

TWELFTH NIGHT 58 | ACT 2 SCENE 3 59

It is the early hours of the morning, Sir Toby and Sir Andrew are enjoying themselves. Feste enters, commenting that the three of them are drunk. Sir Andrew praises Feste's excellent singing and jesting earlier in the evening.

Scene 3

1 Sir Toby, returning home drunk in the early hours of the morning, advises Sir Andrew that it is good to be up early: '*diluculo surgere*' [*saluberrimum est*] to rise early is very healthy.

Olivia's House
Enter SIR TOBY and SIR ANDREW

SIR TOBY Approach, Sir Andrew. Not to be a-bed after midnight is to be up betimes; and 'diluculo surgere', thou know'st –

SIR ANDREW Nay, by my troth, I know not; but I know, to be up late is to be up late.

Extra summaries

... need for a balanced way of life ... our elements, earth, air, fire and water) ... vinced by Sir Andrew that life really ... nd drink.

SIR TOBY A false conclusion. I hate it as an unfilled can. To be ... go to bed then, is early; so ... dnight is to go to bed ... consist of the four

Grading 3

10

SIR ANDREW Faith, so they say; but I think it rather consists of eating and drinking.

SIR TOBY Thou'rt a scholar; let us therefore eat and drink.

3 Feste ...
two a...

TWELFTH NIGHT 32 | ACT 1 SCENE 5 33

Malvolio declares that Feste will not be funny until he suffers the confusion of old age. He seems to criticize Olivia when he suggests that only a fool would laugh at a jester such as Feste. Olivia rebukes Malvolio for being selfish and getting things out of proportion. Maria announces the arrival of Cesario, who has been detained by Sir Toby.

4 Sir An
the en

Infirmity...fool: suffering, which hurts someone of sense and sensitivity, can only be good for a fool
no fox: not sly – the antithesis here suggests that Malvolio is out of his guard: unable to defend himself
minister...him: give him an opportunity as, for example, a 'straight person' feeds lines to a comedian
zanies: clowns who assist a fool
free: innocently generous
bird-bolts: small flat-headed arrows for bird shooting
There is no...nothing but reprove: a licensed fool (Feste) may use abusive language without doing harm while criticism from a trusted adviser (Malvolio) should not be considered abuse
Mercury endue thee with leasing: Mercury, the god of cheats and liars, give you the gift of lying
him...he (line 105): i.e. Sir Toby

5 Feste
given
mone

Infirmity, that decays the wise, doth ever make the better fool.

FESTE God send you, sir, a speedy infirmity, for the better increasing your folly. Sir Toby will be sworn that I am no fox; but he will not pass his word for twopence that you are no fool.

Grading 1

Malvolio?   80
... takes delight in such a barren ... own the other day with an ordinary fool that has no more brain than a stone. Look you now, he's out of his guard already; unless you laugh and minister occasion to him, he is gagged. I protest I take these wise men, that crow so at these set kind of fools, no better than the fools' zanies.

OLIVIA O, you are sick of self-love, Malvolio, and taste with a distempered appetite. To be generous,   90 guiltless, and of free disposition, is to take those things for bird-bolts that you deem cannon-bullets. There is no slander in an allowed fool, though he do nothing but rail; nor no railing in a known discreet man, though he do nothing but reprove.

FESTE Now Mercury endue thee with leasing, for thou speakest well of fools.

Enter MARIA

MARIA Madam, there is at the gate a young gentleman much desires to speak with you.

OLIVIA From the Count Orsino, is it?   100

MARIA I know not, madam: 'tis a fair young man, and well attended.

OLIVIA Who of my people hold him in delay?

MARIA Sir Toby, madam, your kinsman.

OLIVIA Fetch him off, I pray you; he speaks nothing but

Notes

Grading 2

Activities

After every few scenes there is a section containing things to do, helping you to focus on the scenes you have just read:
- questions to make sure you have understood the story
- discussion points about the themes and characters of the play
- drama activities
- character work
- close study to help you understand the language of the play
- writing activities.

Shakespeare's theatre

Heavens the roof above the stage, supported by pillars. Characters could be lowered to the stage during the play.

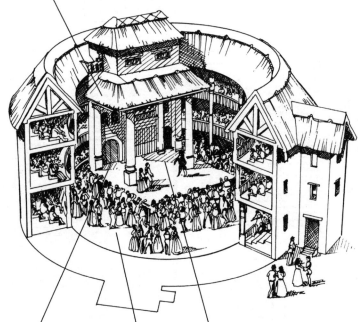

Doors used by the actors, leading from the stage to the tiring house (dressing rooms)

Stage the acting area was very big and had trapdoors so that actors could enter from underneath the stage

Standing space for audience ('groundlings')

Below is a scene from *Twelfth Night* showing both the inner stage and the gallery in use for the action of the play.

When you have studied the play, you should be able to work out exactly which moment in the play this shows.

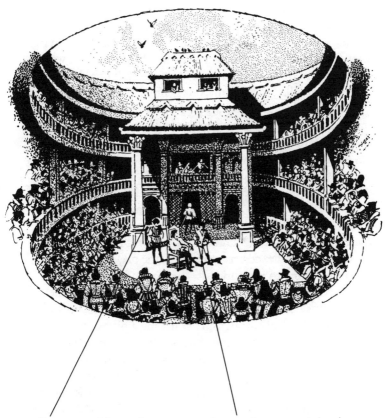

Gallery used for action on an upper level (or, if not, for musicians)

Inner stage curtained area that could be opened up to show a new scene

Going to the theatre in Shakespeare's day

Theatre-going was very popular in Elizabethan London, but it was very different from going to a play today. It was like a cross between going to a football match and going to the theatre. The playhouses were open air and the lack of artificial lighting meant that plays were performed in daylight, normally in the afternoon.

Places were not reserved, so people had to arrive in plenty of time – often more than an hour before the play was due to start. They paid a penny to get into the playhouse, so it was not cheap, since a penny was about one twelfth of a day's wages for a skilled workman. Your penny let you into the large open yard surrounding the stage. The audience here had to stand, looking up at the actors (the stage was 1.5–1.8 metres above the ground). If people wanted a seat, then they had to pay another penny or twopence. This gave admission to the tiers of seating surrounding the yard, and also meant that you had a roof over your head, in case it started to rain. People with even more money could pay to have a seat in an enclosed room. So people of all incomes and social classes attended the theatre and paid for the kind of accommodation they wanted.

While the audience was waiting for the play to begin, people had time to meet friends, talk, eat and drink – in fact they used to continue to enjoy themselves in this way while the play was being performed. But Elizabethan audiences were knowledgeable and enthusiastic. Watching a play was an exciting experience; although the stage was very big, the theatre was quite small, so no-one was far from the actors. When an actor had a **soliloquy** (solo speech) he could come right into the middle of the audience and speak his thoughts in a natural, personal way. At the other extreme the large stage and the three different levels meant that whole battles could be enacted, complete with cannon fire, thunder and lightning and loud military music.

There was no painted stage scenery, so that the audience had to use their imagination to picture the location of each scene, but Shakespeare always gave plenty of word clues in the characters' speeches of when and where a scene took place. The lack of scenery to move about also meant that scene could follow scene without any break. On the other hand, the theatre companies spared no expense on costumes and furniture and other properties; plays also had live music performed by players placed either in the auditorium close to the stage, or in the gallery above it, if that was not to be used in the play.

Altogether Londoners especially must have considered that going to the theatre was an exciting and important part of their lives; it is believed that up to a fifth of them went to the theatre regularly. Shakespeare and the company in which he became a shareholder, the Lord Chamberlain's Men, worked hard and became wealthy.

Sometimes theatre companies gave private performances. *Twelfth Night* can be performed in any large hall and does not necessarily need a gallery or inner stage. We know that it was performed during a feast at the Middle Temple (one of the Inns of Court where lawyers lived and were trained), in February 1602. Later it was performed at the royal court. The title of the play (which refers to January 6, the last day of the Christmas season) suggests that it was first performed as part of private Christmas festivities. It is very likely that once *Twelfth Night* had proved a success with aristocratic and scholarly audiences it was performed for the public.

The characters of the play

ORSINO, Duke of Illyria, with his attendants,

dreams of love …

Valentine and Curio

Orsino

The twins, VIOLA and SEBASTIAN, have been shipwrecked. Though each thinks that the other drowned they have been rescued and have arrived separately in Illyria. Sebastian has been befriended by ANTONIO while Viola, disguised in identical clothes to her brother and calling herself CESARIO, makes her way to Orsino's court.

Antonio

Sebastian

Viola, dressed as Cesario

Maria

Orsino sends Cesario to woo OLIVIA on his behalf.
Olivia is attended by MARIA, her waiting-gentlewoman.

Olivia falls in love with 'Cesario' – but 'Viola' has already fallen for Orsino!

Olivia

At Olivia's house, intent on having a good time, are SIR TOBY BELCH, SIR ANDREW AGUECHEEK – his foolish friend, FABIAN – a servant, and FESTE – Olivia's jester.

Sir Toby Belch

Feste

They loathe MALVOLIO, Olivia's puritanical steward, whom they trick into wearing absurdly inappropriate clothes.

Fabian

Sir Andrew Aguecheek

Olivia is convinced that Malvolio has become mad. He is imprisoned and visited by Feste, disguised as SIR TOPAS, a priest.

Priest

Malvolio

The story of the play

Act 1

Orsino, the Duke of Illyria, is head-over-heels in love with the lady **Olivia**, but she doesn't love him. Olivia, who is mourning the recent death of her brother, is refusing to accept any male visitors. Her parents are dead, too, and she lives with her servants: **Malvolio**, her steward, responsible for the management of her estates; **Maria**, her gentlewoman, a personal servant; **Feste**, the jester, employed to entertain her, and **Fabian**, another servant. Also living in Olivia's house is **Sir Toby Belch**, a relative, who is mainly interested in eating, drinking and having fun. He enjoys the company of Maria but loathes the puritanical Malvolio. Sir Toby has invited his rich but foolish friend, **Sir Andrew Aguecheek**, to stay. Sir Toby has promised Sir Andrew that Olivia will marry him. Everyone except Sir Andrew knows that this is a ridiculous idea, but Sir Toby has been cheating Sir Andrew out of his money and so is keen to continue the pretence.

Meanwhile **Viola** and **Sebastian**, identical twins, have been shipwrecked off the coast of Illyria. They, like Olivia, are orphans. Viola believes that Sebastian has been drowned, though the sea captain who rescues her assures her that he last saw her brother swimming for land, supported by wreckage. Feeling vulnerable and alone, Viola decides to disguise herself in male clothes (of the kind that her brother usually wore) and make her way to Orsino's court where she hopes to gain employment.

Thus disguised, and calling herself Cesario, Viola is welcomed by Orsino. He sends Cesario to Olivia to woo her on his behalf, convinced that Cesario's youthful good looks and attractive speech will persuade Olivia to listen to his declaration of love.

At Olivia's house relationships are not running smoothly. Maria and Olivia tell Feste off for being absent without permission but, when Malvolio sourly criticizes the jester, Olivia stands up for Feste and shows impatience with Malvolio. Cesario arrives and is met first by a drunken Sir Toby and then by starchy Malvolio. When Olivia hears that her visitor is apparently a handsome young man who will not take 'no' for an answer she agrees to see him. In the battle of words which follows Olivia again refuses to listen to Orsino's declaration of love but finds herself attracted by Cesario. When Cesario leaves she sends Malvolio with a ring which, she pretends, Cesario had given to her. She invites Cesario to return the following day, knowing that the youth will do so if only to return the ring.

Act 2

Sebastian, twin brother to Viola, is discovered on his way to Orsino's court. He has been saved from the shipwreck by **Antonio**. Both men believe that Viola was drowned. Antonio has great affection for Sebastian but is reluctant to accompany him any further since he has enemies at Orsino's court.

When Viola, disguised as 'Cesario', receives Olivia's ring and message from Malvolio she is distressed to realize that Olivia has fallen in love with her. Her concern is all the greater because Viola knows that she herself has fallen in love with Orsino.

Late the same night Sir Toby, Sir Andrew and Feste are having a noisy party in Olivia's house. They disturb Malvolio who threatens to report them to Olivia and have them thrown out. Angered by Malvolio they decide to take revenge. Maria devises a plan to convince Malvolio that Olivia is in love with him. She will write a love letter which will seem to be from Olivia and plant it where he will find it.

The following day Orsino is desperately unhappy at his failure to win the affection of Olivia. In conversation with Cesario he argues that men love more deeply and faithfully than women. Cesario disagrees and almost gives her true identity, and her love, away. The Duke sends her once again to Olivia.

Meanwhile, Sir Toby, Sir Andrew and Fabian hide in a box hedge to see Malvolio find Maria's letter and fall completely into the trap set for him. The letter tells him that Olivia loves him and that she wishes him to wear yellow stockings, cross-gartered. He should smile incessantly, be surly with servants and uncivil towards Sir Toby if he is to have greatness 'thrust upon him'. To the delight and fury of the conspirators, Malvolio assumes that it is his destiny to marry Olivia and that he must behave as the letter instructs him.

Act 3

Viola, still disguised as Cesario, returns to Olivia. On the way she meets Feste who impresses her with the wisdom contained in his jesting. Though Sir Toby and Sir Andrew intercept Cesario, Olivia insists on seeing the youth on her own. Olivia confesses her love for Cesario but is rejected.

Observing Olivia's behaviour towards Cesario, Sir Andrew is convinced that he has no hope of marrying her. Sir Toby and Fabian convince him that Olivia is merely using Cesario to make him jealous and that Sir Andrew must challenge Cesario to a duel. Maria reports that Malvolio has followed the ridiculous advice contained in the letter.

Sebastian has arrived in the vicinity of Orsino's court and, despite his fears, Antonio is still with him. They agree that Sebastian will do some sightseeing while Antonio hides in their lodgings. He gives Sebastian all his money in case the young man should want to buy any souvenirs.

When Olivia observes Malvolio's dress and behaviour she is appalled, assuming that he has gone mad. When she hears that Cesario has returned she places Malvolio in the care of Sir Toby, Maria and Fabian, who persist in treating him as if he were possessed by a devil. This only infuriates Malvolio further. They decide to imprison him.

Sir Andrew returns having written an absurd challenge to Cesario. Sir Toby takes the challenge and tells Sir Andrew to hide in order to ambush Cesario. He then tells Cesario that Sir Andrew wishes to kill him and that he is a courageous and dangerous swordsman. While Fabian makes sure that Cesario does not run away, Sir Toby goes to Sir Andrew and tells him that Cesario is fierce and cunning. Fabian and Sir Toby bring the reluctant, fearful duellists together and they prepare to fight. Suddenly Antonio appears, sees Cesario and mistakes him for Viola's identical twin, Sebastian. He offers to fight on

Cesario's behalf but Sir Toby draws his sword to stop him. At this moment Orsino's officers arrive to arrest Antonio who once fought in a sea battle against the Illyrians and so is a wanted man. The threatened duel is stopped but Antonio now asks Cesario for the money he had lent him. The request makes no sense to Viola but when she hears herself addressed as Sebastian she realizes that this could be evidence of her brother's survival. Antonio is taken away to prison. Viola leaves in a hurry and Sir Andrew follows, believing Cesario to be a coward and determined to beat him.

Act 4

Sir Andrew, with Sir Toby and Fabian in pursuit, comes across Sebastian talking to Feste. Sir Andrew naturally mistakes Sebastian for Cesario and strikes him. Sebastian beats Sir Andrew, and Feste goes to fetch Olivia. Sir Toby and Sebastian draw their swords but Olivia arrives, dismisses Sir Toby and apologizes to Sebastian whom she too believes to be Cesario. Sebastian is astonished to be invited home by the beautiful lady.

Feste disguises himself as a priest, 'Sir Topas', and goes to speak to the imprisoned Malvolio. In fact the disguise is unnecessary since Malvolio cannot see out of his dark cell. However, Malvolio can hear the priest, and he does his best to convince Sir Topas that he is not mad. Sir Topas will not be persuaded. When Feste reverts to his usual role as jester he agrees to fetch ink, paper and a light so that Malvolio can write a letter of explanation to Olivia.

Sebastian enters in a complete daze. He has lost Antonio but has been given a jewel by Olivia who now proposes a ceremony of betrothal to him as a prelude to their marriage. Sebastian agrees.

Act 5

Orsino confronts Antonio who says that the only reason he has come to Illyria is to be with his friend. Viola, disguised as Cesario, acknowledges Antonio's offer to fight Sir Andrew but claims that she had never seen him before that moment. Antonio, still mistaking Cesario for Sebastian, is astonished at this apparent betrayal. Olivia enters and, thinking that she has just become betrothed to Cesario, is surprised to find him consorting with the Duke. In the ensuing argument Olivia produces the priest who has witnessed the betrothal. It is Viola's turn to be amazed and she is even more puzzled when Sir Andrew and Sir Toby enter, claiming to have been injured by her.

The comic confusion is reaching its height when Sebastian enters and the twins appear on stage together for the first time. Everyone is amazed but it is some time before Sebastian sees Viola. Slowly the twins tell their stories and begin to realize that the person each thought was dead is alive. Olivia finds herself betrothed to Sebastian and Orsino realizes that Viola loves him. Feste enters with Malvolio's letter and Olivia sends for her steward. Orsino realizes that his affection for the boy Cesario can become love for Viola and offers to marry her. When Malvolio appears Fabian tells the truth of the plot against him. Malvolio swears revenge against everyone and storms out. The Duke proclaims a double wedding: he will marry Viola and Olivia will marry Sebastian. All leave the stage except for Feste who sings a bitter-sweet song which reminds the audience that the play is only fantasy and a cheerful distraction from the rigours of real life.

Shakespeare's fantasy world

At the end of the play Feste reminds us that we have to go out of the theatre and back into a less happy world. There are other moments in the play where characters are overcome with sadness, pain and the problems of dealing with realistic emotions. However, the play is essentially a joyful fantasy and full of impossibilities. For example:

- grown adults are shown behaving like unruly children
- there are no parents to tell any of the lovers what to do
- the behaviour of the lovers as they fall in and out of love is irrational
- the story of the play is absurd – it seems unlikely that Viola could disguise herself so successfully as a man and that she and her brother could be mistaken for each other
- the one apparently serious and responsible person,

Malvolio, is actually a hypocrite, has an appalling trick played upon him and is rejected by almost every other character.

In fact the world of *Twelfth Night* is a world turned upside down. Shakespeare's audience would have recognized that the play offers a temporary escape from reality and the playwright offers clear indications that this is what he is doing:

- the title, which has nothing to do with the plot of the play, suggests that this is going to be an entertainment suitable for that time of the year, when people traditionally want to play games and tell tales in the warm circle of a glittering fire
- the sub-title – 'What You Will' – invites us to take the story any way we want and certainly not to treat it too seriously
- one of the key characters is Feste, a clown or jester. Jesters were allowed to make fun of everyone, regardless of their social position. As Olivia says, '*There is no slander in an allowed fool.*'

TWELFTH NIGHT
OR WHAT YOU WILL

CHARACTERS

ORSINO, Duke of Illyria

VALENTINE
CURIO } gentlemen attending on the duke

1ST OFFICER
2ND OFFICER } in the service of the duke

VIOLA, a lady, later disguised as Cesario
SEBASTIAN, Viola's twin brother
A CAPTAIN, of Viola's wrecked ship, who befriends her
ANTONIO, another sea captain, friend of Sebastian

OLIVIA, a countess
MARIA, Olivia's waiting-woman
SIR TOBY BELCH, Olivia's kinsman
SIR ANDREW AGUECHEEK, companion to Sir Toby
MALVOLIO, Olivia's steward
FABIAN, a member of Olivia's household
FESTE, the clown, Olivia's jester
SERVANT to Olivia
PRIEST

Musicians, lords, sailors, attendants

Orsino is desperately in love with Olivia. He is listening to
music which, at first, fills him with passion. His mood
changes and he tires of the music. Curio suggests that he
should go hunting but Orsino says that he himself is a
hunted animal, pursued by his love for Olivia.

---

excess: too much

surfeiting: over-eating, to the point of self-disgust

strain...fall: drops to a sweet conclusion

Stealing...odour: which draws the scent from the flowers and
allows us to smell them

quick and fresh: keen and hungry

O spirit...in a minute: Love! What a keen appetite you have.
Like the sea, you devour everyone who comes in your way.
Orsino continues the musical image with '*pitch*' but he also
introduces a metaphor from the courtly pursuit of falconry:
'*pitch*' is the highest point of the bird's flight; '*abatement*' is
when it flutters from the perch, attempting to escape.

So full...fantastical: love creates images in the mind: it is the
most imaginative and unreal of conditions

hart: deer, but also a pun on heart

purged: cleansed

pestilence: plague, disease

That instant...pursue me: Orsino refers to the myth of Diana
and the huntsman Actaeon who, when he spied the naked
goddess bathing, was metamorphosed by her into a deer and
destroyed by his own hounds. The story symbolizes
hopeless, destructive love.

fell: ruthless

Act one

Scene 1

The Duke's Palace
Music. Enter ORSINO, *Duke of Illyria,* CURIO, *and other Lords*

DUKE

personed lived of imagination

If music be the food of love, play on,
Give me excess of it; that, <u>surfeiting</u>,
The appetite may sicken, and so die.
That strain again – it had a dying fall.
O, it came o'er my ear like the sweet sound
That breathes upon a bank of violets,
Stealing and giving odour. Enough, no more,
'Tis not so sweet now as it was before.
O spirit of love, how quick and fresh art thou,
That, notwithstanding thy capacity   10
Receiveth as the sea, nought enters there,
Of what validity and pitch soe'er,
But falls into abatement and low price,
Even in a minute! So full of shapes is fancy,
That it alone is high fantastical.

e Something unwanted, comes upon ppl unexpectedly, + easy 2 void.

CURIO   Will you go hunt, my lord?

DUKE   What, Curio?

CURIO   The hart.

DUKE   Why so I do, the noblest that I have.
O when mine eyes did see Olivia first,
Methought she purged the air of pestilence.   20
That instant was I turned into a hart,
And my desires, like fell and cruel hounds,
E'er since pursue me.

Enter VALENTINE

Valentine brings a message from Olivia. She says that, since she is mourning her brother's death, she will see no-one for seven years. This merely assures Orsino of her ability to love passionately.

So please…admitted: I'm sorry but she wouldn't let me in
element: air
The element…view: seven hot summers will pass before she will unveil her face to the open sky
cloistress: nun
eye-offending brine: tears
season: preserve (as food is preserved by seasoning it in salt water)
of that fine frame: so well made
rich golden shaft: Cupid's arrow which, Orsino hopes, will make Olivia love only him and will kill other distracting feelings within her
when liver…king: when Olivia's passion, reason and emotion are all centred on me. (The liver was the 'seat' of passion, the brain the seat of reason and the heart the seat of love, in each of which Orsino hopes to see himself enthroned like a king.)
canopied with bowers: overhung with trees. Orsino is adopting the traditional pose of the desolate lover.

Viola arrives in Illyria.

Illyria: what is now Slovenia and northern Croatia, but Shakespeare chooses the name because it sounds exotic and, perhaps, because it suggests the delirium which will be experienced by many of the characters
Elysium: heaven

How now, what news from her?

VALENTINE So please my lord, I might not be admitted,
But from her handmaid do return this answer:
The element itself, till seven years' heat,
Shall not behold her face at ample view;
But like a cloistress she will veiled walk,
And water once a day her chamber round
With eye-offending brine; all this to season   30
A brother's dead love, which she would keep
    fresh
And lasting, in her sad remembrance.

DUKE O she that hath a heart of that fine frame
To pay this debt of love but to a brother,
How will she love, when the rich golden shaft
Hath killed the flock of all affections else
That live in her; when liver, brain, and heart,
These sovereign thrones, are all supplied and
    filled,
Her sweet perfections, with one self king.
Away before me to sweet beds of flowers: 40
Love-thoughts lie rich when canopied with
    bowers.

[*Exeunt*

Scene 2

A Sea Coast
Enter VIOLA, *a Captain, and Sailors*

VIOLA What country, friends, is this?

CAPTAIN This is Illyria, lady.

VIOLA And what should I do in Illyria?
My brother he is in Elysium.

Viola wonders whether or not her brother was drowned in the same shipwreck from which she has been saved. She rewards the captain when he tells her that he saw her brother clinging to wreckage. Viola hears that Orsino governs Illyria and is in love with Olivia.

Perchance: perhaps, by chance

Most...peril: fortunately helped by God at the moment of danger

teaching...practice: showing him what to do

lived: floated

Arion: a poet and musician who escaped death by being carried ashore on the back of a dolphin which had been charmed by his song

hold acquaintance with: know as friends

Mine own escape...like of him: my survival and your story both encourage me to hope that he survived

in nature as in name: his honourable and courteous personality matches his aristocratic title and family

very late: recently

murmur: rumour

What great...prattle of: whatever the ruling class do the common people will chatter about it

	Perchance he is not drowned – what think you, sailors?
CAPTAIN	It is perchance that you yourself were saved.
VIOLA	O my poor brother, and so perchance may he be.
CAPTAIN	True, madam, and to comfort you with chance,

CAPTAIN   True, madam, and to comfort you with chance,
Assure yourself, after our ship did split,
When you and those poor number saved with
    you   10
Hung on our driving boat, I saw your brother,
Most provident in peril, bind himself –
Courage and hope both teaching him the practice –
To a strong mast that lived upon the sea;
Where, like Arion on the dolphin's back,
I saw him hold acquaintance with the waves
So long as I could see.

VIOLA   For saying so, there's gold.
Mine own escape unfoldeth to my hope,
Whereto thy speech serves for authority,   20
The like of him. Know'st thou this country?

CAPTAIN   Ay, madam, well, for I was bred and born
Not three hours' travel from this very place.

VIOLA   Who governs here?

CAPTAIN   A noble duke, in nature as in name.

VIOLA   What is his name?

CAPTAIN   Orsino.

VIOLA   Orsino – I have heard my father name him.
He was a bachelor then.

CAPTAIN   And so is now, or was so very late;   30
For but a month ago I went from hence,
And then 'twas fresh in murmur – as, you know,
What great ones do the less will prattle of –
That he did seek the love of fair Olivia.

VIOLA   What's she?

CAPTAIN   A virtuous maid, the daughter of a count

Viola is told that Olivia's father and brother have both died within the last year. Olivia will not now meet any man. Viola thinks she would like to join Olivia but when the captain tells her that this is impossible she asks for his help in disguising herself as a young man. She proposes to offer Orsino her services as a musician.

---

abjured: sworn to renounce or give up

And might not... What my estate is: I would wish to keep my identity and social position secret until I think the time is ripe

were...compass: will be hard to bring about

suit: request

There is...pollution: you have behaved well, Captain, and though people are not always what they seem to be...

character: appearance

I prithee: please (I pray thee)

bounteously: very generously

Conceal me what I am: conceal who I really am

as haply....my intent: that, with luck, will suit my intention

eunuch: a man who had been castrated before puberty in order to preserve his unbroken singing voice

allow: prove

What else...to my wit: I'll wait and see what happens; you must keep my secret

mute: a silent servant. The captain ironically refers to the tongueless slaves and eunuchs who guarded the medieval Turkish harem.

	That died some twelvemonth since, then leaving	
	her	
	In the protection of his son, her brother,	
	Who shortly also died; for whose dear love,	
	They say, she hath abjured the company	40
	And sight of men.	

VIOLA   O that I served that lady
And might not be delivered to the world,
Till I had made mine own occasion mellow
What my estate is.

CAPTAIN   That were hard to compass,
Because she will admit no kind of suit,
No, not the Duke's.

VIOLA   There is a fair behaviour in thee, captain,
And though that nature with a beauteous wall
Doth oft close in pollution, yet of thee
I will believe thou hast a mind that suits   50
With this thy fair and outward character.
I prithee – and I'll pay thee bounteously –
Conceal me what I am, and be my aid
For such disguise as haply shall become
The form of my intent. I'll serve this duke;
Thou shalt present me as an eunuch to him
It may be worth thy pains, for I can sing
And speak to him in many sorts of music
That will allow me very worth his service.
What else may hap to time I will commit,   60
Only shape thou thy silence to my wit.

CAPTAIN   Be you his eunuch, and your mute I'll be.
When my tongue blabs, then let mine eyes not
     see.

VIOLA   I thank thee. Lead me on.

                                          [Exeunt

Sir Toby complains about Olivia's behaviour. Maria, his friend and Olivia's servant, tells him that he must come home earlier and drink less. They argue about Sir Andrew, a rich fool whom Sir Toby has encouraged to woo Olivia.

niece: Sir Toby is not Olivia's uncle: she calls him cousin. Both 'niece' and 'cousin' were used imprecisely in the sixteenth century. Sir Toby and Olivia are members of the same family but their exact relationship is not made clear.

care's...life: grief kills

By my troth: honestly

except before excepted: ignore those things which have been ignored in the past

confine yourself...order: not allow your behaviour to get out of hand: Sir Toby puns on the word's two meanings: keep within and dress up

An they be not: if they are not

straps: boot laces, garters

as tall a man as any's: of high social status and good character, with a probable pun on Sir Andrew's lanky build

What's that...purpose?: What do you mean?

three thousand ducats a year: his annual income was a thousand pounds a year. Its buying power would be the equivalent of half a million pounds today.

a prodigal: he throws his money away

Fie: rubbish!

viol-de-gamboys: viola da gamba: a large instrument of the violin family supported on the player's legs

almost natural: a born fool

Scene 3

Olivia's House
Enter SIR TOBY BELCH *and* MARIA

SIR TOBY   What a plague means my niece to take the death of
her brother thus? I am sure care's an enemy to
life.

MARIA   By my troth, Sir Toby, you must come in earlier o'
nights: your cousin, my lady, takes great exceptions
to your ill hours.

SIR TOBY   Why, let her except before excepted.

MARIA   Ay, but you must confine yourself within the
modest limits of order.

SIR TOBY   Confine? I'll confine myself no finer than I am.   10
These clothes are good enough to drink in, and so
be these boots too. An they be not, let them hang
themselves in their own straps.

MARIA   That quaffing and drinking will undo you. I heard
my lady talk of it yesterday; and of a foolish knight
that you brought in one night here to be her wooer.

SIR TOBY   Who, Sir Andrew Aguecheek?

MARIA   Ay, he.

SIR TOBY   He's as tall a man as any's in Illyria.

MARIA   What's that to the purpose?   20

SIR TOBY   Why, he has three thousand ducats a year.

MARIA   Ay, but he'll have but a year in all these ducats: he's
a very fool and a prodigal.

SIR TOBY   Fie, that you'll say so! He plays o' the viol-de-
gamboys, and speaks three or four languages word
for word without book, and hath all the good gifts
of nature.

MARIA   He hath indeed, almost natural; for besides that he's

Maria suggests that Sir Andrew has no good qualities but is stupid, quarrelsome and a drunkard. Sir Andrew enters and makes a fool of himself.

---

and but...grave: his talent for cowardice is as great as his enjoyment of quarrelling; otherwise, sensible people believe, he would be dead by now

substractors: Sir Toby means detractors – those who slander Sir Andrew. The word he uses is an archaic variation of 'subtract' and allows Maria to then make the play on 'add'.

coistrel: rogue

parish top: a large spinning top, the whipping of which was a country sport

Castiliano vulgo: the meaning is now uncertain but is possibly 'talk of the devil'

fair shrew: pretty little creature, alluding both to Maria's small size and suggesting she is bad-tempered. Sir Andrew proclaims his stupidity by this greeting.

Accost: greet courteously

'accost': Sir Toby knows that the word is derived from the action of a boat going alongside to be boarded

front: confront

in this company: in front of the audience

An thou...again: if you let her leave now, Sir Andrew, you will lose all right to be considered a gentleman

	a fool, he's a great quarreller; and but that he hath the gift of a coward to allay the gust he hath in 30 quarrelling, 'tis thought among the prudent he would quickly have the gift of a grave.
SIR TOBY	By this hand, they are scoundrels and substractors that say so of him. Who are they?
MARIA	They that add, moreover, he's drunk nightly in your company.
SIR TOBY	With drinking healths to my niece. I'll drink to her as long as there is a passage in my throat and drink in Illyria. He's a coward and a coistrel that will not drink to my niece till his brains turn o' the toe 40 like a parish top. What, wench! Castiliano vulgo; for here comes Sir Andrew Agueface.

Enter SIR ANDREW AGUECHEEK

SIR ANDREW	Sir Toby Belch! How now, Sir Toby Belch?
SIR TOBY	Sweet Sir Andrew!
SIR ANDREW	[*to* MARIA] Bless you, fair shrew.
MARIA	And you too, sir.
SIR TOBY	Accost, Sir Andrew, accost.
SIR ANDREW	What's that?
SIR TOBY	My niece's chambermaid.
SIR ANDREW	Good Mistress Accost, I desire better 50 acquaintance.
MARIA	My name is Mary, sir.
SIR ANDREW	Good Mistress Mary Accost –
SIR TOBY	You mistake, knight: 'accost' is front her, board her, woo her, assail her.
SIR ANDREW	By my troth, I would not undertake her in this company. Is that the meaning of 'accost'?
MARIA	Fare you well, gentlemen.
SIR TOBY	An thou let part so, Sir Andrew, would thou

Maria makes fun of Sir Andrew. He doesn't really understand her jokes at his expense but he decides that his visit is fruitless and he will return to his own home.

Marry, but: well! ('*Marry*' is a mild exclamation, derived from the oath 'by the Virgin Mary'. Its meaning depends entirely on the context in which it is used.)

thought is free: I can think what I like

buttery-bar: the buttery, where food and drink is stored, had a half-door with a ledge on which to rest tankards and plates

dry: the beginning of a series of puns on the meanings of dry: thirsty, sarcastic, mean, stupid, emotionally cold

I am not...hand dry: a reference to the proverb 'Fools have wit enough to come in out of the rain'

barren: jest(er)-less

canary: sweet, sherry-like, wine from the Canary Islands

put down: outwitted, dead drunk

a Christian or an ordinary man: average human being

beef: being a heavy meat was supposed to dull thought, though it increased courage

Pourquoi: why?

bestowed: spent

tongues: foreign languages

bear-baiting: a cruel sport in which the onlookers gambled on the outcome of a contest between a tethered bear and hunting dogs. There was a bear-baiting pit adjacent to Shakespeare's Globe Theatre.

| | mightst never draw sword again. | 60 |

SIR ANDREW — An you part so, mistress, I would I might never draw sword again. Fair lady, do you think you have fools in hand?

MARIA — Sir, I have not you by the hand.

SIR ANDREW — Marry, but you shall have, and here's my hand.

MARIA — Now, sir, 'thought is free'. I pray you bring your hand to the buttery-bar, and let it drink.

SIR ANDREW — Wherefore, sweetheart? What's your metaphor?

MARIA — It's dry, sir.

SIR ANDREW — Why, I think so: I am not such an ass but I   70 can keep my hand dry. But what's your jest?

MARIA — A dry jest, sir.

SIR ANDREW — Are you full of them?

MARIA — Ay, sir, I have them at my fingers' ends. Marry, now I let go your hand, I am barren.   [*Exit*

SIR TOBY — O knight, thou lack'st a cup of canary. When did I see thee so put down?

SIR ANDREW — Never in your life, I think, unless you see canary put me down. Methinks sometimes I have no more wit than a Christian or an ordinary man has; but I   80 am a great eater of beef, and I believe that does harm to my wit.

SIR TOBY — No question.

SIR ANDREW — An I thought that, I'd forswear it. I'll ride home tomorrow, Sir Toby.

SIR TOBY — Pourquoi, my dear knight?

SIR ANDREW — What is 'pourquoi' – do or not do? I would I had bestowed that time in the tongues that I have in fencing, dancing, and bear-baiting. O, had I but followed the arts.   90

SIR TOBY — Then hadst thou had an excellent head of hair?

SIR ANDREW — Why, would that have mended my hair?

Sir Toby appears to flatter Sir Andrew and assures him that Olivia will have nothing to do with Orsino. Sir Andrew decides to stay for another month. He remarks that he enjoys all kinds of entertainment and is an especially good dancer.

---

flax on a distaff: flax, from which linen cloth is made, would hang straight and yellow. The distaff is a long rod on which it is spun. The phrase gives a forceful description of Sir Andrew's hair or wig and his physical proportions.

a housewife...spin it off: Sir Toby hopes to see Sir Andrew driven hairless as a result of marriage. '*Housewife*' also meant 'prostitute' from which he might catch a sexually transmitted disease and thus (according to contemporary belief) lose his hair.

Count: Orsino – called a Duke in the stage directions and speech headings but usually referred to as Count in the text. A duke is higher in rank than a count, but count is not a British title. Shakespeare may have intended to indicate that Orsino held two titles, or may simply not have bothered to correct the prompter's copy of the play.

match above...wit: marry outside her social class and age group, or someone who has greater wealth and understanding.

degree: social position

there's life in't: as the proverb, while there's life there's hope.

masques and revels: dramatic performances, fun and games

kickshawses: trifles – from French, *quelque chose*: something

under...betters: as long as he is not better than I am

galliard: a quick dance in which one step was a leap or 'caper'

cut the mutton: a pun on capers which are also used in making a sauce to accompany mutton

back-trick: a reverse of the caper.

Mistress Mall's picture: probably a topical allusion, now obscure.

coranto: another type of quick dance

sink-a-pace: cinquepace – a dance with five steps, like a galliard. Sink also means sewer: a vulgar play on words.

formed...galliard: your horoscope at your birth showed you were destined to be a great dancer.

SIR TOBY	Past question; for thou seest it will not curl by nature.
SIR ANDREW	But it becomes me well enough, does't not?
SIR TOBY	Excellent; it hangs like flax on a distaff, and I hope to see a housewife take thee between her legs and spin it off.
SIR ANDREW	Faith, I'll home tomorrow, Sir Toby. Your niece will not be seen, or if she be, it's four to one 100 she'll none of me: the Count himself here hard by woos her.
SIR TOBY	She'll none o' the Count; she'll not match above her degree, neither in estate, years, nor wit; I have heard her swear't. Tut, there's life in't, man.
SIR ANDREW	I'll stay a month longer. I am a fellow o' the strangest mind i' the world; I delight in masques and revels sometimes altogether.
SIR TOBY	Art thou good at these kickshawses, knight?
SIR ANDREW	As any man in Illyria, whatsoever he be, under 110 the degree of my betters; and yet I will not compare with an old man.
SIR TOBY	What is thy excellence in a galliard, knight?
SIR ANDREW	Faith, I can cut a caper.
SIR TOBY	And I can cut the mutton to 't.
SIR ANDREW	And I think I have the back-trick simply as strong as any man in Illyria.
SIR TOBY	Wherefore are these things hid? Wherefore have these gifts a curtain before 'em? Are they like to take dust, like Mistress Mall's picture? Why 120 dost thou not go to church in a galliard and come home in a coranto? My very walk should be a jig. I would not so much as make water but in a sink-a-pace. What dost thou mean? Is it a world to hide virtues in? I did think, by the excellent constitution of thy leg, it was formed under the star of a galliard.

They agree that they were both born to enjoy themselves and Sir Toby demonstrates Sir Andrew's foolishness by having him dance extravagant steps as he leaves the stage.

---

damned coloured stock: '*stock*' is short for 'stockings', but 'damned' is either a gratuitous oath or a mistake

set...revels: have a party

Taurus: each of the signs of the zodiac was associated with a different part of the body. Taurus governed the neck and the throat. Sir Andrew is wrong to associate the sign with the chest. Sir Toby pretends that it governs the leg in order to make his friend dance ridiculously.

ACTIVITIES

Keeping track

Scene 1

1 What does the Duke do in this scene?
2 What is Valentine's news about Olivia and how does Orsino respond to it?

Scene 2

3 Why is Viola upset?
4 What is Viola's reaction to the Captain's news of Olivia?
5 What does Viola decide at the end of the scene?

Scene 3

6 What does Maria object to in Sir Toby's behaviour?

Discussion

1 In the first few minutes of a play we must learn quickly who some of the most important characters are and what they are doing.

SIR ANDREW	Ay, 'tis strong, and it does indifferent well in a damned coloured stock. Shall we set about some revels?	
SIR TOBY	What shall we do else? Were we not born under Taurus?	130
SIR ANDREW	Taurus? That's sides and heart.	
SIR TOBY	No, sir; it is legs and thighs. Let me see thee caper. Ha! higher! Ha, ha! excellent!	

[Exeunt

- Look at the list of characters on page 1.
- Which characters have we met or heard about so far?
- Which scene is each of the characters in?
- Why do you think Shakespeare arranges these three scenes in the order he does?
- Which characters would you expect to meet in the next couple of scenes?

2 The beginning of the play also establishes a mood and atmosphere.
  - What is the atmosphere of the first scene?
  - If you were producing a modern-dress version of the play what piece of music would you choose for the Duke to be listening to at the beginning of the play?
  - How does the mood of the second scene compare and contrast with scene 1? For example, what differences can you detect between the behaviour of Orsino and Olivia in these scenes?
  - Scene 3 is designed to make the audience laugh. What is comic about the behaviour of Sir Toby, Maria and Sir Andrew?

3 Both Olivia and Viola are grieving (and both for the death of brother).
   • What practical effects might the deaths of their brothers have on them?
   • Would other people expect them to behave any differently?

Drama

1 **Who's who**
   The Duke says that 'fancy' is '*so full of shapes...that it alone is high fantastical.*'(Act 1 scene 1 lines 14–15). The play is set in the never-neverland of Illyria and over the years designers and directors have translated this world into many different places and times. Recently companies have tended to concentrate on costume more than set, preferring to let the words create the place.
   • Work in groups of three or four.
   • Read again the first three scenes.
   • Look for clues about the appearance and dress of the main characters.
   • Make some drawings of costumes for Orsino, Viola, Sir Toby and Sir Andrew.

2 Read the first exchanges between Sir Toby, Sir Andrew and Maria.
   • Work in groups of three or four.
   • Make notes describing the kind of actors you would need to play these parts. Look for evidence in the text and write it down.
   • Select actors who are in current film or television drama to suit the roles.

3 Imagine Valentine and Curio have a conversation about Duke Orsino in private.
   • Role-play the conversation they have, showing what they think of the Duke's behaviour with regard to Olivia.
   • Discuss what happened in your role play. What did you learn about the Duke's personality and his suitability as a ruler?

Follow up
Write a script of the scene you developed in your role play.

Characters

1 Start to keep a CHARACTER LOG on all the main characters.
Instructions for this are to be found on page 206. You will be
able to add the first entries for Orsino, Viola, Sir Toby, Sir
Andrew and Maria.

Orsino

2 What is your impression of Orsino? How would you describe
his behaviour and his attitude to women?

Viola

3 Thinking carefully about what we learn of the Captain's
character in scene 2, write the diary entry he might make
about the shipwreck, about Viola and her decisions.
4 What do we learn of Viola's background? Why, do you think,
she feels drawn to Olivia? What does Viola say which illustrates
her basic generosity and kindness?

Sir Toby, Sir Andrew and Maria

5 Sir Toby is a knight and related to Olivia. In what ways is his
behaviour inappropriate to his social status? Why do you think
his last name is 'Belch'?
6 Sir Andrew is called 'Aguecheek'. Find out what 'ague' means
and suggest why his name is appropriate. In what ways do you
think Sir Toby and Sir Andrew differ from each other?
7 What is Maria's relationship with, and opinion of, Sir Andrew?
She has a sharp tongue and a dry sense of humour. Find some
examples of these.

Close study

Scene 1 lines 1–15

1 What evidence is there that the Duke can quickly change his

mind and his mood?

2 Look carefully at lines 1–3 and 7–8. What do these lines suggest about his love?

The whole scene

3 List the comparisons (**similes** and **metaphors**) that Orsino uses? What do they tell us about him and his attitude to love?

Writing

1 Valentine says:

'*So please my lord, I might not be admitted,*
But from her handmaid do return this answer'

Imagine Valentine's meeting with Olivia's handmaid, Maria. Script their conversation, trying to reflect what you know of their behaviour, manner and characters.

2 Viola has now chosen to be in disguise. We know a little about her character but as soon as she puts on a costume she may begin to behave differently. She will appear to be a young man – which is bound to affect the way she moves, thinks and talks.

   • Imagine you had to disguise yourself, perhaps as someone of the opposite sex, in order to escape from a dangerous situation.
   • Write a description of your disguise.
   • When you put on the disguise how does it make you feel?
   • What sort of behaviour or actions would be made easier by your disguise and why would this be the case?
   • Write a story about what happens when you put the disguise on.

3 Maria writes to a close friend about Sir Toby and Sir Andrew. Write this letter, including what she thinks of the two of them and what she thinks they are up to.

4 Write the article published in *Illyria Illustrated* which gives an account of the shipwreck and the people involved in it. Include extracts from the 'Gossip Column', which will feature news of recent comings and goings at court and news of the aristocracy. Mention Viola and her brother, Orsino, Sir Toby

and Sir Andrew.

5 Imagine that Sir Toby writes two letters describing Sir Andrew. One he sends to Olivia. The other, an honest one, he sends to one of his old drinking partners who now lives at the other end of Illyria. Write the two letters. Try to use a different style for each of them. Remember:

- He really wants to impress Olivia with Sir Andrew's abilities.
- He is staying free of charge with Olivia so he must not say anything to upset her, in case she sends him away.
- He is much more intelligent than Sir Andrew and despises his stupidity.

Quiz

1 For how long does Olivia intend to remain in mourning?
2 Where does Orsino go to when he wants to think about love?
3 How long is it since Olivia's father and brother died?
4 What, according to Sir Toby, is 'an enemy to life'?
5 Who doesn't understand the meaning of the word 'accost'?
6 Whose hair is causing him trouble?
7 What, apart from drinking, seems to be Sir Andrew's only talent?

Viola, now disguised as Cesario, has been servant to
Orsino for three days and is, according to Valentine, being
treated as a favourite. Orsino commands that, since he has
told Cesario the extent of his love for Olivia, the young
man must woo her on Orsino's behalf. Cesario must speak
to Olivia whether or not the lady wants to see him. [Note:
from this point onwards the summaries refer to Viola as
Cesario except when she is speaking as herself in
soliloquies and asides.]

his humour or my negligence: his state of mind or my poor
service
Thou know'st...soul: you know everything. I have even
revealed to you the deepest secrets of my heart.
address thy gait unto: walk to
thy fixed...audience: your feet will take root (at her front
door) until she listens to your message from me
abandoned...spoke: entirely preoccupied by her mourning as
the rumours suggest
Be clamorous...return: make loud demands and go beyond
the bounds of good manners rather than return to me
without having spoken to her

Scene 4

The Duke's Palace
Enter VALENTINE, *and* VIOLA *as* CESARIO, *in man's attire*

VALENTINE   If the Duke continue these favours towards you, Cesario, you are like to be much advanced. He hath known you but three days, and already you are no stranger.

VIOLA   You either fear his humour or my negligence, that you call in question the continuance of his love. Is he inconstant, sir, in his favours?

VALENTINE   No, believe me.

Enter DUKE, CURIO, *and Attendants*

VIOLA   I thank you. Here comes the Count.

DUKE   Who saw Cesario, ho?   10

VIOLA   On your attendance, my lord, here.

DUKE   [*To Curio and Attendants*] Stand you a while aloof. [*To Viola*] Cesario,
Thou know'st no less but all. I have unclasped
To thee the book even of my secret soul.
Therefore, good youth, address thy gait unto her;
Be not denied access, stand at her doors,
And tell them, there thy fixed foot shall grow
Till thou have audience.

VIOLA   Sure, my noble lord,
If she be so abandoned to her sorrow
As it is spoke, she never will admit me.   20

DUKE   Be clamorous and leap all civil bounds,
Rather than make unprofited return.

VIOLA   Say I do speak with her, my lord, what then?

DUKE   O, then unfold the passion of my love,

Orsino is sure that Cesario's youthful appearance and wise words will convince Olivia. If successful, Orsino will give Cesario anything he wishes – but Viola wants nothing but to marry Orsino.

Surprise...faith: capture her affections by speaking of my intense, honest love

nuncio's of more grave aspect: older messenger's

For they...a man: for those who say you are a man do no justice to your fortunate youthful appearance

Diana: the beautiful goddess of chastity

thy small...organ: your voice is unbroken like a girl's

semblative a woman's part: as if you were playing the role of a woman

thy constellation is right apt: your horoscope suggests you are the right person

live as freely...thine: I'll give you anything you want

a barful strife: an almost impossible task – with a play on 'strife' which suggests both hard labour and Viola's war within herself

At Olivia's house Maria rebukes Feste the jester for going absent without leave.

FESTE: he is described as a clown, a fool and a jester. These titles imply that he was in the tradition of court entertainers who were allowed great freedom to criticize and make fun of everyone, from the monarch down, and were expected to sing, tell stories and amuse. However outrageous his behaviour the jester was unlikely to be punished but his continued employment depended upon him pleasing his employer.

fear no colours: fear no enemy, with a pun on colours, collars and cholers (anger)

Make that good: prove it

a good lenten answer: a weak reply; your wit must have been fasting during Lent

Surprise her with discourse of my dear faith.
It shall become thee well to act my woes;
She will attend it better in thy youth
Than in a nuncio's of more grave aspect.

VIOLA   I think not so, my lord.

DUKE   Dear lad, believe it;
For they shall yet belie thy happy years,   30
That say thou art a man. Diana's lip
Is not more smooth and rubious; thy small pipe
Is as the maiden's organ, shrill of sound,
And all is semblative a woman's part.
I know thy constellation is right apt
For this affair. Some four or five attend him.
All, if you will, for I myself am best
When least in company. Prosper well in this,
And thou shalt live as freely as thy lord,
To call his fortunes thine.

VIOLA   I'll do my best   40
To woo your lady. [*Aside*] Yet, a barful strife.
Whoe'er I woo, myself would be his wife.

                                              [*Exeunt*

Scene 5

Olivia's House
Enter MARIA *and* FESTE

MARIA   Nay, either tell me where thou hast been, or I will
                not open my lips so wide as a bristle may enter in
                way of thy excuse. My lady will hang thee for thy
                absence.

FESTE   Let her hang me. He that is well hanged in this
                world needs to fear no colours.

MARIA   Make that good.

FESTE   He shall see none to fear.

MARIA   A good lenten answer. I can tell thee where that

Feste will not account for his absence and Maria tells him he may be dismissed. He jests with her, compliments her wit and implies that he knows something about her relationship with Sir Toby. Olivia enters and attempts to dismiss Feste since he is dishonest and no longer funny.

for turning…out: as for my being sacked, wait and see
two points: laces which attached a man's breeches (gaskins, trousers which ended below the knee) to his doublet
piece of Eve's flesh: woman
Peace you rogue, no more o' that: Maria is suddenly embarrassed when Feste suggests she may have influence over Sir Toby

1 Feste is suddenly unsure of himself as he meets Olivia. She commands his removal.

	saying was born, of 'I fear no colours'. 10
FESTE	Where, good Mistress Mary?
MARIA	In the wars; and that may you be bold to say in your foolery.
FESTE	Well, God give them wisdom that have it; and those that are fools, let them use their talents.
MARIA	Yet you will be hanged for being so long absent; or to be turned away, is not that as good as a hanging to you?
FESTE	Many a good hanging prevents a bad marriage; and, for turning away, let summer bear it out. 20
MARIA	You are resolute, then?
FESTE	Not so neither, but I am resolved on two points.
MARIA	That if one break, the other will hold; or if both break, your gaskins fall.
FESTE	Apt, in good faith, very apt. Well, go thy way – if Sir Toby would leave drinking, thou wert as witty a piece of Eve's flesh as any in Illyria.
MARIA	Peace you rogue, no more o' that. Here comes my lady: make your excuse wisely, you were best.

[Exit

| FESTE | Wit, an't be thy will, put me into good fooling.   30 Those wits that think they have thee do very oft prove fools; and I that am sure I lack thee may pass for a wise man. For what says Quinapalus? 'Better a witty fool than a foolish wit.' |

Enter Lady OLIVIA *with* MALVOLIO *and* ATTENDANTS

	God bless thee, lady!
OLIVIA	Take the fool away.
FESTE	Do you not hear, fellows? Take away the lady.
OLIVIA	Go to, you're a dry fool; I'll no more of you. Besides, you grow dishonest.

2 ⟩

Feste plays on words to prove that a combination of drink and her good advice will make him a better fool. Olivia, however, is the greater fool because, argues Feste, she continues to mourn a dead brother when she should rejoice that he is in heaven. Olivia seems to like Feste's answer.

---

2 He attempts to convince her that no-one is perfect: all are patched like the jester's motley garment, so all are fools.

Misprision: mistake
'Cucullus non facit monachum': a monk's cowl (hood) doesn't make the man into a monk
motley: the jester's traditional chequered costume
madonna: my lady
Dexteriously: dexterously, precisely
catechize: question (as in a set of questions used by the Church to teach Christian doctrine to children)
mouse of virtue: honest little thing
bide: wait for
mend: improve

FESTE	Two faults, madonna, that drink and good 40 counsel will amend: for give the dry fool drink, then is the fool not dry: bid the dishonest man mend himself; if he mend, he is no longer dishonest; if he cannot, let the botcher mend him. Anything that's mended is but patched: virtue that transgresses is but patched with sin, and sin that amends is but patched with virtue. If that this simple syllogism will serve, so; if it will not, what remedy? As there is no true cuckold but calamity, so beauty's a flower. The lady bade take away the fool, therefore, I say 50 again, take her away.
OLIVIA	Sir, I bade them take away you.
FESTE	Misprision in the highest degree. Lady, 'Cucullus non facit monachum'; that's as much to say as I wear not motley in my brain. Good madonna, give me leave to prove you a fool.
OLIVIA	Can you do it?
FESTE	Dexteriously, good madonna.
OLIVIA	Make your proof.
FESTE	I must catechize you for it, madonna. Good my 60 mouse of virtue, answer me.
OLIVIA	Well, sir, for want of other idleness, I'll bide your proof.
FESTE	Good madonna, why mournest thou?
OLIVIA	Good fool, for my brother's death.
FESTE	I think his soul is in hell, madonna.
OLIVIA	I know his soul is in heaven, fool.
FESTE	The more fool, madonna, to mourn for your brother's soul being in heaven. Take away the fool, gentlemen. 70
OLIVIA	What think you of this fool, Malvolio? Doth he not mend?
MALVOLIO	Yes, and shall do till the pangs of death shake him.

Malvolio declares that Feste will not be funny until he suffers the confusion of old age. He seems to criticize Olivia when he suggests that only a fool would laugh at a jester such as Feste. Olivia rebukes Malvolio for being selfish and getting things out of proportion. Maria announces the arrival of Cesario, who has been detained by Sir Toby.

Infirmity...fool: suffering, which hurts someone of sense and sensitivity, can only be good for a fool

no fox: not sly – the antithesis here suggests that Malvolio is

out of his guard: unable to defend himself

minister...him: give him an opportunity as, for example, a 'straight person' feeds lines to a comedian

zanies: clowns who assist a fool

free: innocently generous

bird-bolts: small flat-headed arrows for bird shooting

There is no...nothing but reprove: a licensed fool (Feste) may use abusive language without doing harm while criticism from a trusted adviser (Malvolio) should not be considered abuse

Mercury endue thee with leasing: Mercury, the god of cheats and liars, give you the gift of lying

him...he (line 105): i.e. Sir Toby

Infirmity, that decays the wise, doth ever make the
better fool.

FESTE   God send you, sir, a speedy infirmity, for the better
increasing your folly. Sir Toby will be sworn that I
am no fox; but he will not pass his word for
twopence that you are no fool.

OLIVIA   How say you to that, Malvolio?   80

MALVOLIO   I marvel your ladyship takes delight in such a barren
rascal. I saw him put down the other day with an
ordinary fool that has no more brain than a stone.
Look you now, he's out of his guard already; unless
you laugh and minister occasion to him, he is
gagged. I protest I take these wise men, that crow
so at these set kind of fools, no better than the
fools' zanies.

OLIVIA   O, you are sick of self-love, Malvolio, and taste with
a distempered appetite. To be generous,   90
guiltless, and of free disposition, is to take those
things for bird-bolts that you deem cannon-bullets.
There is no slander in an allowed fool, though he
do nothing but rail; nor no railing in a known
discreet man, though he do nothing but reprove.

FESTE   Now Mercury endue thee with leasing, for thou
speakest well of fools.

             Enter MARIA

MARIA   Madam, there is at the gate a young gentleman
much desires to speak with you.

OLIVIA   From the Count Orsino, is it?   100

MARIA   I know not, madam: 'tis a fair young man, and well
attended.

OLIVIA   Who of my people hold him in delay?

MARIA   Sir Toby, madam, your kinsman.

OLIVIA   Fetch him off, I pray you; he speaks nothing but

Olivia sends Maria both to rescue Cesario from Sir Toby and to refuse the youth entry. Sir Toby enters drunk and unable to speak coherently. Olivia sends Feste to look after him.

a suit: courtship
Jove: Jupiter, greatest of the Roman gods
weak pia mater: weak brain, poor head for drink

3 Sir Toby enters in a drunken state and Olivia accuses him. Unable to understand her or tell her who has arrived he staggers off.

3 ▷

4 The clown comments that drunkenness has three stages: foolishness, madness and death. Olivia thinks Sir Toby has reached the third stage and they will need the coroner to convene an inquest.

4 ▷

madman. Fie on him! [*Exit Maria*] Go you,
Malvolio. If it be a suit from the Count, I am sick,
or not at home – what you will to dismiss it. [*Exit Malvolio*] Now you see, sir, how your fooling grows
old, and people dislike it.   110

FESTE   Thou hast spoke for us, madonna, as if thy eldest
son should be a fool; whose skull Jove cram with
brains, for – here he comes – one of thy kin has a
most weak pia mater.

Enter SIR TOBY

OLIVIA   By mine honour, half drunk. What is he at the gate,
cousin?

SIR TOBY   A gentleman.

OLIVIA   A gentleman? What gentleman?

SIR TOBY   'Tis a gentleman here [*he belches*] – a plague o' these
pickle-herring! How now, sot!   120

FESTE   Good Sir Toby –

OLIVIA   Cousin, cousin, how have you come so early by this
lethargy?

SIR TOBY   Lechery? I defy lechery. There's one at the gate.

OLIVIA   Ay, marry, what is he?

SIR TOBY   Let him be the devil an he will, I care not; give me
faith, say I. Well, it's all one.
                                                            [*Exit*

OLIVIA   What's a drunken man like, fool?

FESTE   Like a drowned man, a fool and a madman: one
draught above heat makes him a fool; the   130
second mads him; and a third drowns him.

OLIVIA   Go thou and seek the coroner, and let him sit o' my
coz; for he's in the third degree of drink, he's
drowned. Go, look after him.

FESTE   He is but mad yet, madonna, and the fool shall look
to the madman.   [*Exit*

Malvolio tells Olivia that Cesario will not take 'No' for an answer. When she hears that Cesario is good-looking and very young she tells Malvolio to admit him. She prepares to see him in the company of Maria and with her face veiled.

5

5 Malvolio returns to say that Viola will not be persuaded to go away.

a sheriff's post: a post erected at the sheriff's door to which public notices were fixed
supporter to a bench: as solid as a chair leg
will you or no: whether you wish to or not
personage: physical appearance
squash: unripe pea-pod (peascod)
codling: unripe apple
standing water: at the turn of the tide
well-favoured: handsome
shrewishly: like a sharp-tongued woman
embassy: message delivered by his ambassador

Enter MALVOLIO

MALVOLIO	Madam, yond young fellow swears he will speak with you. I told him you were sick; he takes on him to understand so much, and therefore comes to speak with you. I told him you were asleep; he 140 seems to have a foreknowledge of that too, and therefore comes to speak with you. What is to be said to him, lady? He's fortified against any denial.
OLIVIA	Tell him he shall not speak with me.
MALVOLIO	He's been told so; and he says he'll stand at your door like a sheriff's post, and be the supporter to a bench, but he'll speak with you.
OLIVIA	What kind o' man is he?
MALVOLIO	Why, of mankind. 150
OLIVIA	What manner of man?
MALVOLIO	Of very ill manner. He'll speak with you, will you or no.
OLIVIA	Of what personage and years is he?
MALVOLIO	Not yet old enough for a man, nor young enough for a boy; as a squash is before 'tis a peascod, or a codling when 'tis almost an apple. 'Tis with him in standing water, between boy and man. He is very well-favoured and he speaks very shrewishly. One would think his mother's milk were scarce out 160 of him.
OLIVIA	Let him approach. Call in my gentlewoman.
MALVOLIO	Gentlewoman, my lady calls. [*Exit*

Re-enter MARIA

OLIVIA	Give me my veil: come, throw it o'er my face. We'll once more hear Orsino's embassy.

Enter VIOLA *as* CESARIO

VIOLA	The honourable lady of the house, which is she?

Olivia will not tell Cesario whether she is indeed the lady he wishes to speak to. Cesario says that he won't speak until he is sure that he is addressing Olivia; nor will he say anything other than Orsino's message, which he has learnt by heart. Olivia confirms her identity but refuses to listen to flattery. She tells Cesario to be brief or be gone.

---

penned: composed

con: learn

I am...usage: I am sensitive to the smallest criticism

out of my part: not one of the speeches I have been asked to learn

give me modest assurance: tell me, as befits a lady of your gentility

comedian: actor (since you will only speak the words you have been given)

No, my profound heart: not in my heart of hearts

by the very fangs of malice: by the devil (represented as a serpent)

I am not that I play: – doubly ironic since a male actor is playing the part of a woman who is disguised as a man

usurp myself: pretend to be what I already am

what is...reserve: you may not keep for yourself that which you have a duty to give to others

from my commission: not in my message

feigned: fiction

'tis not...with me: I'm not mad enough; I'm not in the mood. Madness – lunacy – was thought to be connected with the moon's phases. There may also be a reference to a woman's menstrual cycle and its associated changes of mood.

make one...dialogue: join you in such wild talk

swabber: one who washes the decks

to hull: to keep my sails furled

OLIVIA	Speak to me, I shall answer for her. Your will?
VIOLA	Most radiant, exquisite, and unmatchable beauty – I pray you, tell me if this be the lady of the house, for I never saw her. I would be loath to cast away 170 my speech; for besides that it is excellently well penned, I have taken great pains to con it. Good beauties, let me sustain no scorn; I am very comptible, even to the least sinister usage.
OLIVIA	Whence came you, sir?
VIOLA	I can say little more than I have studied, and that question's out of my part. Good gentle one, give me modest assurance if you be the lady of the house, that I may proceed in my speech.
OLIVIA	Are you a comedian? 180
VIOLA	No, my profound heart. And yet, by the very fangs of malice I swear, I am not that I play. Are you the lady of the house?
OLIVIA	If I do not usurp myself, I am.
VIOLA	Most certain, if you are she, you do usurp yourself; for what is yours to bestow is not yours to reserve. But this is from my commission. I will on with my speech in your praise, and then show you the heart of my message.
OLIVIA	Come to what is important in 't. I forgive you 190 the praise.
VIOLA	Alas, I took great pains to study it, and 'tis poetical.
OLIVIA	It is the more like to be feigned; I pray you, keep it in. I heard you were saucy at my gates, and allowed your approach rather to wonder at you than to hear you. If you be not mad, be gone; if you have reason, be brief; 'tis not that time of moon with me to make one in so skipping a dialogue.
MARIA	Will you hoist sail, sir? Here lies your way.
VIOLA	No, good swabber, I am to hull here a little 200

Maria tries to have Cesario removed and Olivia accuses him of rudeness. He replies that he was only responding to his reception by Sir Toby. Cesario insists on speaking to Olivia alone; when she grants this he persuades her also to take off her veil. He praises her beauty.

mollification...giant: make peace with your protector (whose small size Viola alludes to)

overture: declaration

taxation of homage: claim that you are Orsino's servant

olive: olive branch – a symbol of peace

The rudeness...profanation: my apparent bad manners have been taught me by my greeting (from Malvolio, Sir Toby and Olivia). What I am and what I should like to be are an unbreakable secret. What I have to say is a sacred truth for your ears only; to anyone else the words would be sinful.

divinity: sacred truth, sermon. Olivia plays on the metaphor that the words of love which Viola has learnt are like an expression of religious truth and she pretends that they take the form of a sermon which would begin with a text from a chapter of the Bible. A sermon should teach correct doctrine; if it does not this would be heresy. (This kind of extended metaphor is called a conceit.)

such a one...present: this is what I am and always have been

if God did all: if you aren't wearing make-up

in grain: part of me

	longer. Some mollification for your giant, sweet lady. Tell me your mind. I am a messenger.
OLIVIA	Sure, you have some hideous matter to deliver, when the courtesy of it is so fearful. Speak your office.
VIOLA	It alone concerns your ear. I bring no overture of war, no taxation of homage; I hold the olive in my hand. My words are as full of peace as matter.
OLIVIA	Yet you began rudely. What are you? What would you? 210
VIOLA	The rudeness that hath appeared in me have I learned from my entertainment. What I am, and what I would, are as secret as maidenhead – to your ears, divinity; to any others' profanation.
OLIVIA	Give us the place alone; we will hear this divinity. [*Exit Maria and Attendants*] Now, sir, what is your text?
VIOLA	Most sweet lady –
OLIVIA	A comfortable doctrine, and much may be said of it. Where lies your text? 220
VIOLA	In Orsino's bosom.
OLIVIA	In his bosom? In what chapter of his bosom?
VIOLA	To answer by the method, in the first of his heart.
OLIVIA	O, I have read it; it is heresy. Have you no more to say?
VIOLA	Good madam, let me see your face.
OLIVIA	Have you any commission from your lord to negotiate with my face? You are now out of your text; but we will draw the curtain and show you the picture. [*Unveiling*] Look you, sir, such a one I 230 was this present. Is't not well done?
VIOLA	Excellently done, if God did all.
OLIVIA	'Tis in grain, sir, 'twill endure wind and weather.

Cesario tells Olivia that such beauty as hers should be preserved through her having children. Olivia promises, instead, to have her description published. Cesario speaks of Orsino's love but Olivia says that she cannot love him, despite his nobility, honour and good looks. Cesario cannot understand why Olivia will not love Orsino. Were she Orsino she would camp on Olivia's doorstep.

---

blent: blended

cunning: skilful

the cruell'st she: the cruellest woman

If you...copy: if you intend to die without having children to inherit your beauty

divers schedules: many lists

inventoried...will: listed, and every detail attached to my will (so that I can leave my beauty to my heirs in the same way that I leave my property)

I see...fair: – an allusion to Satan, the beautiful angel whose pride caused him to rebel against God

O, such...beauty: it would only be a fair reward for Orsino's love if you loved him in return, even if you were considered the most beautiful of women

nonpareil of: incomparable

fertile: continual

stainless: perfect

In voices...free: spoken well of, generous

in dimension...nature: in his physical appearance

what would you: what would you do?

willow cabin: a wooden hut; willow was the symbol of unhappy love

my soul: my beloved – Olivia

VIOLA	'Tis beauty truly blent, whose red and white
	Nature's own sweet and cunning hand laid on.
	Lady, you are the cruell'st she alive,
	If you will lead these graces to the grave,
	And leave the world no copy.

OLIVIA
O, sir, I will not be so hard-hearted. I will give out
divers schedules of my beauty. It shall be   240
inventoried, and every particle and utensil labelled
to my will: as – item, two lips, indifferent red; item,
two grey eyes, with lids to them; item, one neck,
one chin, and so forth. Were you sent hither to
praise me?

VIOLA
I see what you are, you are too proud;
But, if you were the devil, you are fair.
My lord and master loves you. O, such love
Could be but recompensed, though you were
        crowned
The nonpareil of beauty.

OLIVIA   How does he love me?   250

VIOLA
With adorations, fertile tears,
With groans that thunder love, with sighs of fire.

OLIVIA
Your lord does know my mind; I cannot love him.
Yet I suppose him virtuous, know him noble,
Of great estate, of fresh and stainless youth;
In voices well divulged, free, learned, and valiant;
And in dimension and the shape of nature
A gracious person: but yet I cannot love him.
He might have took his answer long ago.

VIOLA
If I did love you in my master's flame,   260
With such a suffering, such a deadly life,
In your denial I would find no sense;
I would not understand it.

OLIVIA   Why, what would you?

VIOLA
Make me a willow cabin at your gate,
And call upon my soul within the house;

There she would keep Olivia awake by singing love songs
and shouting her name. Olivia asks Cesario about himself
and, having confirmed that he is a gentleman, sends him
away with a message of rejection to Orsino but with an
invitation to Cesario to return. Cesario refuses payment
for delivering his message. When he has gone Olivia
reveals to the audience that she has found him attractive.
She calls for Malvolio.

---

cantons: songs

contemned: condemned, unrequited

Halloo...hills: shout your name so that it echoes round the
hills

the babbling gossip of the air: the echoes, personified in the
nymph Echo

Between...earth: anywhere in the world

Above...well: better than my present condition yet my social
position is still high

fee'd post: paid messenger

Love make...in contempt: Viola hopes that when Olivia loves
someone her love will be unrequited and she will suffer as
Orsino now suffers

five-fold blazon: a coat of arms indicating a family has been in
the higher social ranks for five generations

Unless: if only (Orsino were Cesario)

Even so...eyes: can one catch a disease so quickly? I am catching love for him through my eyes, just as one would breathe
in an invisible illness.

Write loyal cantons of contemned love,
And sing them loud even in the dead of night;
Halloo your name to the reverberate hills
And make the babbling gossip of the air
Cry out 'Olivia!' O, you should not rest   270
Between the elements of air and earth,
But you should pity me.

OLIVIA   You might do much. What is your parentage?

VIOLA   Above my fortunes, yet my state is well:
            I am a gentleman.

OLIVIA   Get you to your lord.
            I cannot love him; let him send no more –
            Unless, perchance, you come to me again
            To tell me how he takes it. Fare you well.
            I thank you for your pains. [*Offers a purse*]
                Spend this for me.

VIOLA   I am no fee'd post, lady; keep your purse.   280
            My master, not myself, lacks recompense.
            Love make his heart of flint that you shall love,
            And let your fervour, like my master's, be
            Placed in contempt. Farewell, fair cruelty.   [*Exit*

OLIVIA   'What is your parentage?'
            'Above my fortunes, yet my state is well:
            I am a gentleman.' I'll be sworn thou art;
            Thy tongue, thy face, thy limbs, actions and spirit,
            Do give thee five-fold blazon – not too fast; soft,
                soft –
            Unless the master were the man. How now?   290
            Even so quickly may one catch the plague?
            Methinks I feel this youth's perfections
            With an invisible and subtle stealth
            To creep in at mine eyes. Well, let it be.
            What ho, Malvolio!

            Enter MALVOLIO

MALVOLIO   Here, madam, at your service.

Olivia pretends that Cesario has left a ring as a present from Orsino. Malvolio is to chase after Cesario, give the ring back but invite the youth to return tomorrow. Olivia places herself in the hands of Fate.

peevish: obstinate
Would I or not: whether I wanted him to or not
flatter with: encourage
fear to find...mind: I am afraid that what I see is making me change my mind
owe: own

ACTIVITIES

Keeping track

Scene 4

1 In the three days since Viola has been at Orsino's court what has happened there?
2 What does Orsino ask Viola to do?
3 Why does Orsino think that Viola is the right person for the job?

Scene 5

4 Why is Feste in trouble?
5 Why does Feste call Olivia a fool?
6 What is Malvolio's attitude to Feste?
7 What is Olivia's reaction to Sir Toby's drunkenness?
8 Why does Olivia allow Cesario to speak to her?
9 What are three signs which show that Olivia wants to encourage Cesario to stay and to speak to her?
10 What would Cesario do, if she were Orsino, in order to woo Olivia (lines 264–272)?

OLIVIA   Run after that same peevish messenger,
         The County's man. He left this ring behind him,
         Would I or not. Tell him I'll none of it.
         Desire him not to flatter with his lord,   300
         Nor hold him up with hopes; I'm not for him:
         If that the youth will come this way tomorrow,
         I'll give him reasons for 't. Hie thee, Malvolio.

MALVOLIO Madam, I will.   [*Exit*

OLIVIA   I do I know not what, and fear to find
         Mine eye too great a flatterer for my mind.
         Fate, show thy force; ourselves we do not owe;
         What is decreed must be; and be this so.   [*Exit*

11 What effect does Cesario have on Olivia and what does Olivia decide to do about it?

Discussion

1 How do the Duke and Viola feel about each other at the end of scene four?
2 Consider all the characters we have been introduced to in Act 1.
   • What complications are beginning to develop in their relationships with each other?
   • What do you think are going to be the main story-lines in the rest of the play?

Drama

1 Look at the exchanges between Maria and Feste in the first 27 lines of scene 5.
   - In pairs work out the moves that these two characters would be making while saying their lines.
   - Think of activities they might be doing. For example, perhaps Maria is hanging out washing. Feste might use the washing to make jokes and hide behind it.
   - How might Maria react to Feste's interruption? Is she flattered by his attention? Does she become really cross or just pretend to be?
2 • Work in pairs.
   - Choose one of Malvolio's two speeches describing Cesario (Act 1 scene 5 lines 137–144 or 155–161).
   - One of you should take the part of Malvolio and the other that of Olivia.
   - How does the pompous Malvolio deliver these lines?
   - How does Olivia receive them?
   - Practise saying the lines. What gestures does each character make?
3 • Work in pairs, one of you being Viola, the other Olivia.
   - Look at the lines where Viola's passion finally breaks through Olivia's indifference (Act 1 scene 5 lines 246–259).
   - Practise saying these lines, making them more passionate with each reading.
   - What movement and gesture might fit with the lines? (For example, does Viola touch Olivia?)
   - Perform the scene to the rest of the class. Decide whether you wish to make your audience laugh at the situation or have sympathy with the characters.

Characters

Orsino

1 How does Orsino feel about Cesario/Viola after three days?
   - What has Orsino told Viola and asked her to do which shows that he trusts the youth?

- Read scene 4 lines 30–39. What has Orsino noticed about Cesario's appearance?
- What effect would his observations in these lines have on an audience?

Olivia

2 We have now seen Olivia. Is there any difference between the woman described in the first four scenes and the one we see in scene 5?
- How does she deal with Feste, Malvolio and Viola?
- What is her response to Viola's flattery?
- Why do you think Shakespeare delays Olivia's appearance on stage?
- Why does Olivia ask Malvolio to give Viola/Cesario the ring?
- What does this suggest about her feelings for Cesario? Try to find quotations that support your point of view.

Viola

3 What evidence is there that Viola is intelligent, charming and resourceful? In what ways does she demonstrate her loyalty to Orsino?

Feste

4 Feste is a professional jester.
- Read the note on page 26 to find out more about him.
- What kinds of things does he do or say that would normally be regarded as insulting or out of place?
- What are his opinions of Malvolio and Olivia?

Malvolio

5 Malvolio arouses strong feelings in people.
- Add him to your CHARACTER LOG.
- What are his strengths and his weaknesses?
- He is described as a puritan: read the note in the middle of page 66 for a definition of this word.

- In what ways is Malvolio a good example of the worst kind of puritan?
- Can you suggest why he is called Malvolio? (Look up malevolent and other words beginning with the prefix 'mal-' to help you.)

Close study

Scene 5 lines 218–294

Read the lines again. You may also find it helpful to do DRAMA activity 3.

1 At line 234 Shakespeare changes from prose to verse (see pages 212 to 214 for explanations of these words) and, apart from a speech by Olivia, the rest of her conversation with Viola is in verse. Why do you think Shakespeare decided to do this?

2 Read Viola's speech: lines 264–272.
- What impression of love does Viola create in this speech?
- What words and images help to create the mood of rejected love in the speech?
- Does the speech tell us anything of Viola's feelings or state of mind?

3 Olivia says: '*Even so quickly may one catch the plague?*' (line 291)
- What is she comparing to '*the plague*'?
- In what ways is this **metaphor** appropriate?
- Compare this to Orsino's reference to the plague ('*pestilence*') in Act 1 scene 1 line 20. In what ways are they using the metaphor to mean very different things? Does the comparison tell us anything about their characters?

Writing

1 Imagine that Valentine, one of Orsino's courtiers, is interviewed by the local newspaper *Illyria Illustrated* about the new courtier, Cesario.
- Role play the interview.
- Repeat the role play and, this time, record it.

- Listen to the recording and choose a short section to use in the newspaper.
- Make a transcript (write out all the words spoken).
- Write the article using some or all of the transcript.

2 In *Illyria Illustrated* there is a series of articles about court life and jobs. Write Feste's short guide for those who want to become a jester.

3 Imagine that Maria writes to a close friend, Olivia's former housekeeper. Write her letter, bearing these points in mind:
- her letters are full of gossip about events in the house
- Maria enjoys these weekly opportunities to discuss scandal and the news
- she has firm ideas about people and the way they should behave.

4 Malvolio, of course, keeps a careful diary. Write three entries from it in which:
- he records his thoughts and feelings
- he reflects upon his job as steward
- he comments upon the people he meets and lives with
- he is brutally honest about his attitude to others
- he is boastful of his own achievements and talents.

5 Write the diary entries that Olivia and Viola might make following their meeting.

Quiz

Who says the following, and to whom?
1 '*Thou know'st no less but all.*'
2 '*Whoe'er I woo, myself would be his wife.*'
3 '*My lady will hang thee for thy absence.*'
4 '*Take away the fool, gentlemen.*'
5 '*O, you are sick of self-love*'
6 '*He is very well-favoured and he speaks very shrewishly.*'
7 '*Farewell, fair cruelty.*'
8 '*ourselves we do not owe.*'

Sebastian is sad and wishes to be alone. He reveals himself as the twin brother of Viola whom he believes drowned in the shipwreck. Antonio has saved Sebastian. Sebastian mourns his twin and says that they looked very much like each other.

Will you...you?: will you neither stay longer nor let me go with you?

My stars...yours: Fate, as demonstrated by my horoscope, is against me and my ill-fortune may affect you

It were...recompense: it would be a poor repayment

sooth: truly

my determinate...extravagancy: I have decided merely to wander

But I perceive...myself: you are too polite to question me about my private plans so I must, for the sake of good manners, tell you something about myself

Roderigo: – Sebastian has been travelling under this false name

Messaline: an imaginary town

in an hour: at the same time

If the...drowned: – Sebastian wishes that, since he believes his sister drowned, Fate had killed him at the same time

the breach of the sea: the breakers

estimable wonder: high esteem – the point being that Sebastian is modestly unwilling to praise her appearance too much since he has already suggested that he closely resembled her

Act two

Scene 1

Near the Sea Coast
Enter ANTONIO *and* SEBASTIAN

ANTONIO   Will you stay no longer, nor will you not that I go
           with you?

SEBASTIAN By your patience, no. My stars shine darkly over
           me; the malignancy of my fate might perhaps
           distemper yours; therefore I shall crave of you
           your leave that I may bear my evils alone. It were
           a bad recompense for your love to lay any of them
           on you.

ANTONIO   Let me yet know of you whither you are bound.

SEBASTIAN No, sooth, sir, my determinate voyage is mere   10
           extravagancy. But I perceive in you so excellent a
           touch of modesty, that you will not extort from me
           what I am willing to keep in; therefore it charges
           me in manners the rather to express myself. You
           must know of me then, Antonio, my name is
           Sebastian, which I called Roderigo. My father was
           that Sebastian of Messaline whom I know you have
           heard of. He left behind him myself and a sister,
           both born in an hour. If the heavens had been
           pleased, would we had so ended. But you, sir,   20
           altered that; for some hour before you took me
           from the breach of the sea was my sister drowned.

ANTONIO   Alas the day!

SEBASTIAN A lady, sir, though it was said she much resembled
           me, was yet of many accounted beautiful. But,
           though I could not with such estimable wonder
           overfar believe that, yet thus far I will boldly publish

Sebastian refuses to allow Antonio to serve him and says that he intends to go to Orsino's court. Antonio cannot follow him since he has enemies there.

she bore...fair: even those who envied her had to admit that she was virtuous

with more: i.e. with more tears

bad entertainment: poor hospitality

If you...servant: Unless you wish me to die of love for you, let me be your servant

If you...me: Sebastian is so moved by his sister's death and Antonio's love that he fears he will cry – '*the manners of my mother*' – or die of a broken heart

danger shall seem sport: I'll take the risk

Malvolio, catching up with Cesario, gives him the ring and Olivia's message.

on a...hither: walking at a normal speed I have only just got here

put your...him: convince Orsino that his desire is hopeless

hardy: brave

come again...affairs: visit again on his behalf

her: she bore a mind that envy could not but call
fair. She is drowned already, sir, with salt water,
though I seem to drown her remembrance   30
again with more.

ANTONIO   Pardon me, sir, your bad entertainment.

SEBASTIAN   O good Antonio, forgive me your trouble.

ANTONIO ⌐   If you will not murder me for my <u>love,</u> let me be
feelin' 4   your servant.
  ↓
SEBASTIAN   If you will not undo what you have done, that is,
kill him whom you have recovered, desire it not.
Fare ye well at once; my bosom is full of kindness,
and I am yet so near the manners of my mother,
that upon the least occasion more mine eyes will 40
tell tales of me. I am bound to the Count Orsino's
court. Farewell.   [*Exit*

ANTONIO   The gentleness of all the gods go with thee.
I have many enemies in Orsino's court,
Else would I very shortly see thee there.
But come what may, I do adore thee so,
That danger shall seem sport, and I will go.   [*Exit*

Scene ② —————————

A Street
Enter VIOLA *as* CESARIO, *and* MALVOLIO

MALVOLIO   Were not you even now with the Countess Olivia?

VIOLA   Even now, sir; on a moderate pace I have since
arrived but hither.

MALVOLIO   She returns this ring to you, sir; you might have
saved me my pains, to have taken it away yourself.
She adds, moreover, that you should put your lord
into a desperate assurance she will none of him. And
one thing more, that you be never so hardy to
come again in his affairs, unless it be to report your

Cesario rejects the ring; Malvolio leaves it on the ground and exits. Viola realizes that the ring is a ploy to ensure that she will return to Olivia who has fallen in love with Cesario. Viola confesses her love for Orsino and despairs at the hopeless triangle she is now in. Only time can resolve the situation.

this: both the message and the ring

Receive it so: take the ring and understand my message

peevishly: ill-temperedly

in your eye: in your sight (on the ground)

made good view of me: got a good look at me; liked what she saw

methought…distractedly: I thought what she saw of me made her tongue-tied and caused her to speak hesitantly

the cunning…messenger: it is her love for me which skilfully uses this ill-mannered messenger to invite me to visit her

I am the man: whom she loves

pregnant enemy: the clever Devil

How easy…their forms: how easy it is for handsome but deceitful men to mould women's affections so that they love such men

fadge: sort itself out

monster: unnatural thing, i.e. man-woman-man

fond, dote: love unthinkingly

thriftless: profitless

	lord's taking of this. Receive it so. 10
VIOLA	She took the ring of me; I'll none of it.
MALVOLIO	Come, sir, you peevishly threw it to her; and her will is it should be so returned. If it be worth stooping for, there it lies in your eye; if not, be it his that finds it. [*Exit*
VIOLA	I left no ring with her. What means this lady?

Fortune forbid my outside have not charmed her,
She made good view of me; indeed so much
That sure methought her eyes had lost her
        tongue,
For she did speak in starts distractedly. 20
She loves me sure; the cunning of her passion
Invites me in this churlish messenger.
None of my lord's ring? Why, he sent her none.
I am the man. If it be so, as 'tis,
Poor lady, she were better love a dream.
Disguise, I see thou art a wickedness
Wherein the pregnant enemy does much.
How easy is it for the proper false
In women's waxen hearts to set their forms.
Alas, our frailty is the cause, not we, 30
For such as we are made of, such we be.
How will this fadge? My master loves her dearly,
And I, poor monster, fond as much on him;
And she, mistaken, seems to dote on me.
What will become of this? As I am man,
My state is desperate for my master's love;
As I am woman, – now alas the day –
What thriftless sighs shall poor Olivia breathe.
O time, thou must untangle this, not I;
It is too hard a knot for me t'untie. 40
                                    [*Exit*

ot human, but –
ot ugly

It is the early hours of the morning. Sir Toby and Sir Andrew are enjoying themselves. Feste enters, commenting that the three of them are fools. Sir Andrew praises Feste's excellent singing and jesting earlier in the evening.

1 Sir Toby, returning home drunk in the early hours of the morning, advises Sir Andrew that it is good to be up early: *'diluculo surgere' [saluberrimum est]* – to rise early is very healthy.

2 Sir Toby argues the need for a balanced way of life (suggested by the four elements, earth, air, fire and water) but he is rapidly convinced by Sir Andrew that life really only requires food and drink.

3 Feste enters and suggests that they look like the picture of two asses entitled '*We Three*', the viewer being the third ass.

4 Sir Andrew praises Feste for his appearance, good voice and the entertaining nonsense he had spoken earlier.

5 Feste thanks him nonsensically for the money Andrew had given him to spend on his mistress. He is given more money for a repeat performance.

Scene 3

Olivia's House
Enter SIR TOBY *and* SIR ANDREW

SIR TOBY   Approach, Sir Andrew. Not to be a-bed after
             midnight is to be up betimes; and 'diluculo
             surgere', thou know'st –

SIR ANDREW   Nay, by my troth, I know not; but I know, to be up
             late is to be up late.

SIR TOBY   A false conclusion. I hate it as an unfilled can. To be
             up after midnight and to go to bed then, is early; so
             that to go to bed after midnight is to go to bed
             betimes. Does not our life consist of the four
             elements?   10

SIR ANDREW   Faith, so they say; but I think it rather consists of
             eating and drinking.

SIR TOBY   Thou'rt a scholar; let us therefore eat and drink.
             Marian, I say, a stoup of wine!

             Enter FESTE

SIR ANDREW   How comes the fool, i' faith.

FESTE   How now, my hearts! Did you never see the picture
             of 'We Three'?

SIR TOBY   Welcome, ass. Now let's have a catch.

SIR ANDREW   By my troth, the fool has an excellent breast. I had
             rather than forty shillings I had such a leg, and   20
             so sweet a breath to sing, as the fool has. In sooth,
             thou wast in very gracious fooling last night, when
             thou spokest of Pigrogromitus, of the Vapians
             passing the equinoctial of Queubus; 'twas very
             good, i' faith. I sent thee sixpence for thy leman –
             hadst it?

FESTE   I did impeticos thy gratillity; for Malvolio's nose is

The knights insist that Feste sing a love song. His lyric comments on the brevity of youth and the need to make the most of love before it is too late. Sir Toby demands that they sing a rowdy part-song.

---

good life: virtuous behaviour: Sir Andrew misunderstands Feste for whom '*good*' here means joyful and careless.

Trip: step

wise man's son: fool, since it was proverbial that wise men have foolish sons

i' faith: in faith, honestly

'Tis not hereafter: it doesn't last…

Youth's…not endure: and nor does youth

stuff: material, commodity; it can also imply something that is ridiculous or pointless as in the phrase 'stuff and nonsense'

mellifluous: sweet-sounding

contagious: catching, but when applied to '*breath*' it suggests a bad smell or disease

To hear…contagion: if we heard through the nose we would call this sweetly smelly

the welkin: the heavens

catch: a round (song)

three souls…weaver: there were many Puritan refugee weavers from the Netherlands in London at the time. Music supposedly had the power to draw out the soul: Sir Toby suggests they sing particularly powerfully.

no whipstock. My lady has a white hand, and the
Myrmidons are no bottle-ale houses.

SIR ANDREW   Excellent! Why, this is the best fooling, when all   30
is done. Now, a song.

SIR TOBY   Come on, there is sixpence for you. Let's have a
song.

SIR ANDREW   There's a testril of me too; if one knight give a –

FESTE   Would you have a love-song, or a song of good life?

SIR TOBY   A love-song, a love-song.

SIR ANDREW   Ay, ay; I care not for good life.

FESTE   [*Sings*]
O mistress mine, where are you roaming?
O stay and hear, your true love's coming,
    That can sing both high and low.   40
Trip no further, pretty sweeting;
Journeys end in lovers meeting,
    Every wise man's son doth know.

SIR ANDREW   Excellent good, i' faith.

SIR TOBY   Good, good.

FESTE   [*Sings*]
What is love? 'Tis not hereafter;
Present mirth hath present laughter;
    What's to come is still unsure.
In delay there lies no plenty,
Then come kiss me, sweet and twenty;   50
    Youth's a stuff will not endure.

SIR ANDREW   A mellifluous voice, as I am true knight.

SIR TOBY   A contagious breath.

SIR ANDREW   Very sweet and contagious, i' faith.

SIR TOBY   To hear by the nose, it is dulcet in contagion. But
shall we make the welkin dance indeed? Shall we
rouse the night-owl in a catch that will draw three
souls out of one weaver? Shall we do that?

They sing a nonsense song which wakes the household. Maria tries to silence them but Sir Toby only sings more drunken fragments. Malvolio arrives and tells them off, even though the knights are his social superiors.

---

dog: good

By'r lady: a mild oath; By Our Lady, i.e the Virgin Mary

knave: rogue

constrained: forced

Hold thy peace: silence!

Catch sung: the catch consists largely of the line '*Hold thy peace, thou knave*' sung as a simple round

Cataian: Cathayan: a Chinaman and thus proverbially untrustworthy

politicians: schemers

Peg-a-Ramsey: scolding woman (though the precise meaning is now lost). Sir Toby seems to suggest that there is little to choose between Olivia, Malvolio and himself.

consanguineous: of the same blood (as Olivia)

Tillyvally: nonsense!

'There...lady': the first line of a ballad, 'Constant Susanna', which could be sung to the tune of 'Greensleeves'

Beshrew me: damn me!

if he be disposed: if he is in the mood

natural: naturally, but the word also means 'idiot'

December: perhaps a drunken error for Christmas and thus a reference to the title of the play

wit: commonsense and understanding

coziers: cobblers

mitigation: reduction

remorse of voice: thought of limiting the pain caused by the loudness of your voice

SIR ANDREW	An you love me, let's do't. I am dog at a catch.
FESTE	By'r lady, sir, and some dogs will catch well. 60
SIR ANDREW	Most certain. Let our catch be, 'Thou knave'.
FESTE	'Hold thy peace, thou knave', knight? I shall be constrained in 't to call thee knave, knight.
SIR ANDREW	'Tis not the first time I have constrained one to call me knave. Begin, fool: it begins 'Hold thy peace'.
FESTE	I shall never begin if I hold my peace.
SIR ANDREW	Good, i' faith. Come, begin. [*Catch sung*

Enter MARIA

MARIA	What a caterwauling do you keep here! If my lady have not called up her steward Malvolio, and bid him turn you out of doors, never trust me. 70
SIR TOBY	My lady's a Cataian, we are politicians, Malvolio's a Peg-a-Ramsey, and [*Sings*] 'Three merry men be we'. Am not I consanguineous? Am I not of her blood? Tillyvally, 'lady' [*Sings*] 'There dwelt a man in Babylon, Lady, lady'.
FESTE	Beshrew me, the knight's in admirable fooling.
SIR ANDREW	Ay, he does well enough if he be disposed, and so do I too; he does it with a better grace, but I do it more natural.
SIR TOBY	[*Sings*] 'O, the twelfth day of December' – 80
MARIA	For the love o' God, peace!

Enter MALVOLIO

MALVOLIO	My masters, are you mad? Or what are you? Have you no wit, manners, nor honesty, but to gabble like tinkers at this time of night? Do ye make an alehouse of my lady's house, that ye squeak out your coziers' catches without any mitigation or remorse of voice? Is there no respect of place,

Malvolio tells Sir Toby that Olivia will allow him to stay at her house only so long as he behaves himself. Sir Toby replies with a drunken song. Malvolio criticizes Maria's behaviour and exits to inform Olivia.

Sneck up: go hang yourself!

round: blunt

harbours...kinsman: gives you hospitality because you are related to her

allied to: in sympathy with or connected to

misdemeanours: offences

[*Sings*]: in the next twelve lines the three now sing their own adaptation of a popular song by Robert Jones: 'Farewell dear love, since thou wilt needs be gone...'

cakes and ale: food and drink particularly associated with the festivities of the twelve days of Christmas and thus despised by Puritans

ginger: used to spice ale and winter foods

Go, sir...crumbs: go away and clean your chain of office

stoup: flagon or tankard

if you...rule: if you valued the friendship and generosity of Olivia at all you would not encourage or provide opportunity for this wild behaviour

by this hand: in writing

Go shake your ears: a rude dismissal of Malvolio implying that he is an ass

persons, nor time in you?

SIR TOBY   We did keep time, sir, in our catches. Sneck up!

MALVOLIO   Sir Toby, I must be round with you. My lady   90
bade me tell you that, though she harbours you as
her kinsman, she's nothing allied to your disorders.
If you can separate yourself and your
misdemeanours, you are welcome to the house; if
not, an it would please you to take leave of her, she
is very willing to bid you farewell.

SIR TOBY   [Sings] 'Farewell, dear heart, since I must needs be
gone.'

MARIA   Nay, good Sir Toby.

FESTE   [Sings] 'His eyes do show his days are almost   100
done.'

MALVOLIO   Is't even so?

SIR TOBY   [Sings] 'But I will never die.'

FESTE   [Sings] Sir Toby, there you lie.

MALVOLIO   This is much credit to you.

SIR TOBY   [Sings] 'Shall I bid him go?'

FESTE   [Sings] 'What an if you do?'

SIR TOBY   [Sings] 'Shall I bid him go, and spare not?'

FESTE   [Sings] 'O no, no, no, no, you dare not.'

SIR TOBY   Out o' tune, sir: ye lie. Art any more than a   110
steward? Dost thou think, because thou art
virtuous, there shall be no more cakes and ale?

FESTE   Yes, by Saint Anne, and ginger shall be hot i' the
mouth too.

SIR TOBY   Thou'rt i' the right. Go, sir, rub your chain with
crumbs. A stoup of wine, Maria!

MALVOLIO   Mistress Mary, if you prized my lady's favour at any
thing more than contempt, you would not give
means for this uncivil rule; she shall know of it, by
this hand.   [Exit   120

MARIA   Go shake your ears.

Sir Toby and his friends discuss how to revenge
themselves on Malvolio. Maria says that she will use his
puritanism against him. His belief in his own virtue leads
him to assume that all who see him, love him. Maria will
write him a love letter.

'Twere as good...fool of him: it's good to drink and just as
good to challenge a man to a duel but not keep the
engagement in order to leave him looking foolish

out of quiet: in need of peace, agitated

gull him...recreation: trick him into public humiliation, a
common laughing stock

do not...my bed: think that I haven't got the sense to make
myself comfortable in bed

Possess us: let us into the secret

puritan: religious killjoy. Shakespeare and other writers of the
time used the word in a negative sense since puritans wished
to see theatres and other forms of public entertainment
forbidden. However, the name is derived from 'pure' and
the puritan's aim was fundamentally to turn the recently
established Church of England to a simpler form of worship
and administration, without bishops, and to base public and
private morality on a strict interpretation of the Bible.

exquisite: precise

time-pleaser: deceiver

affectioned ass: affected fool, poseur

that cons...himself: that learns impressive jargon by heart and
quotes it by the yard; he only impresses himself

grounds of faith: belief

on that...work: because he is vain (thinking that everyone
loves his high moral tone) he will be bound to be deceived
by my strategy for revenge

epistle: letter

manner of his gait: way he walks

most feelingly personated: exactly described

on a forgotten matter: when we find a piece of writing which
we have forgotten we did

SIR ANDREW	'Twere as good a deed as to drink when a man's a-hungry, to challenge him the field, and then to break promise with him and make a fool of him.
SIR TOBY	Do't, knight: I'll write thee a challenge; or I'll deliver thy indignation to him by word of mouth.
MARIA	Sweet Sir Toby, be patient for tonight. Since the youth of the Count's was today with my lady, she is much out of quiet. For Monsieur Malvolio, let 130 me alone with him. If I do not gull him into a nayword, and make him a common recreation, do not think I have wit enough to lie straight in my bed. I know I can do it.
SIR TOBY	Possess us, possess us, tell us something of him.
MARIA	Marry, sir, sometimes he is a kind of puritan.
SIR ANDREW	O, if I thought that, I'd beat him like a dog.
SIR TOBY	What, for being a puritan? Thy exquisite reason, dear knight?
SIR ANDREW	I have no exquisite reason for't, but I have 140 reason good enough.
MARIA	The devil a puritan that he is, or any thing constantly, but a time-pleaser; an affectioned ass, that cons state without book and utters it by great swarths; the best persuaded of himself, so crammed, as he thinks, with excellencies, that it is his grounds of faith that all that look on him love him; and on that vice in him will my revenge find notable cause to work.
SIR TOBY	What wilt thou do? 150
MARIA	I will drop in his way some obscure epistle of love; wherein, by the colour of his beard, the shape of his leg, the manner of his gait, the expressure of his eye, forehead, and complexion, he shall find himself most feelingly personated. I can write very like my lady your niece; on a forgotten matter we

Maria intends that when Malvolio finds the letter he will
believe it was written by Olivia. Maria retires to bed but
the knights stay up to drink. Sir Toby tells Sir Andrew to
provide himself with more ready money if Sir Toby is to
arrange his marriage with Olivia.

---

make...hands: distinguish our handwriting apart
device: clever scheme
I have't: the device (or something else?)
Ass: is a pun on 'as'
Sport royal: entertainment fit for a monarch
physic: medicine
plant: hide
construction: interpretation
Penthesilea: Queen of the Amazons, a mythical race of warrior
    women. The reference is to the '*royal*' sport, Maria's
    sophisticated '*device*' and, ironically, her small size.
beagle: a small dog used for hunting hares
Thou hadst need...money: see Act 1 scene 3 line 21 and
    note. Sir Andrew is being made to pay for Sir Toby's
    friendship and the hope of marriage to Olivia
I am a foul way out: I have lost my way in a quagmire, lost
    my money
cut: a horse, gelding, hence an obscenity
burn some sack: warm some sherry

can hardly make distinction of our hands.

SIR TOBY   Excellent! I smell a device.

SIR ANDREW   I have't in my nose too.

SIR TOBY   He shall think, by the letters that thou wilt drop, 160
              that they come from my niece, and that she's in
              love with him.

MARIA   My purpose is indeed a horse of that colour.

SIR ANDREW   And your horse now would make him an ass.

MARIA   Ass I doubt not.

SIR ANDREW   O, 'twill be admirable!

MARIA   Sport royal, I warrant you. I know my physic will
              work with him. I will plant you two, and let the fool
              make a third, where he shall find the letter; observe
              his construction of it. For this night to bed,   170
              and dream on the event. Farewell.   [*Exit*

SIR TOBY   Good night, Penthesilea.

SIR ANDREW   Before me, she's a good wench.

SIR TOBY   She's a beagle true-bred, and one that adores me.
              What o' that?

SIR ANDREW   I was adored once too.

SIR TOBY   Let's to bed, knight. Thou hadst need send for
              more money.

SIR ANDREW   If I cannot recover your niece, I am a foul way
              out.   180

SIR TOBY   Send for money, knight: if thou hast her not i'
              the end, call me cut.

SIR ANDREW   If I do not, never trust me, take it how you will.

SIR TOBY   Come, come, I'll go burn some sack; 'tis too late to
              go to bed now. Come, knight; come, knight.
                                                      [*Exeunt*

ACTIVITIES

Keeping track

Scene 1

1 Why does Sebastian ask Antonio not to follow him?
2 What does Sebastian tell us about his sister?
3 What does Antonio decide to do at the end of Act 2 scene 1? What difficulties might this decision cause him?

Scene 2

4 What problems (Act 2 scene 2 lines 21–38) does Viola believe that only time can untangle?

Scene 3

5 What are Sir Toby, Sir Andrew and Feste doing after midnight?
6 How does Malvolio respond to their behaviour and with what does he threaten them?
7 How does Maria propose to take revenge upon Malvolio?

Discussion

1 Re-read what Viola says after Malvolio has left the ring with her (scene 2 lines 16–40).
   • What does Viola think about the way women respond to love?
   • How far, do you think, does Shakespeare show an understanding of a woman's experience of love in this speech?
2 We know that Sebastian and Viola look very similar. We also know that Viola is disguised as a young man.
   • What complications and confusions are likely to occur now?
   • Olivia is attracted to Viola. Viola loves Orsino. Orsino loves Olivia. What will happen?

3 How would you describe Malvolio's behaviour? Do you think that his criticisms of all the other inhabitants of Olivia's house are correct?

Drama

All in the mind

Look at Viola's **soliloquy**, scene 2 lines 16–40. (See GLOSSARY, page 235, for an explanation of 'soliloquy'.)

- Working as a whole class, divide up the lines between you so that everyone has at least part of a line.
- Make sure you know who has the line before and after yours.
- Learn your line quickly. Say it to your partner.
- The whole class says the lines out loud. Use only eye contact to indicate who is next.
- One of you or your teacher adopts the role of Viola. The rest of you become the voices in her head. Whisper your lines at her.
- A lot of these lines are questions. How will she move? What might she be doing while these voices nag her?

Characters

Antonio

1 In scene 1 we meet Antonio and Sebastian for the first time. How would you describe their relationship? Re-read Antonio's final speech in this scene. In what way does he change his mind? What does this tell us about his character and his feelings for Sebastian?

Sebastian

2 In what respects, apart from appearance, is Sebastian like his sister? Add him to your CHARACTER LOG.

Viola

3 How does Viola feel about Olivia in scene 2?

Malvolio

4 What do scenes 2 and 3 add to our understanding of Malvolio's character? Does he always tell the truth? In what ways does he show himself to be self-important and rude?

Maria

5 What do we learn of Maria's character, and her relationship with Sir Toby, in scene 3?

Sir Andrew

6 Sir Andrew is unintelligent, easily persuaded and follows Sir Toby's lead in everything. Look at scene 3.
   • Find as many examples as you can of Sir Andrew doing or saying what Sir Toby does or says.
   • What other examples of his stupidity can you find in scene 3?
   • How does Sir Toby persuade him to stay longer?
   • Sir Andrew proposes to challenge Malvolio to a duel and then walk out on him. What does this tell us about his character?
   • Sir Andrew says, '*I was adored once too.*' Why is this line funny and sad at the same time?

Close study

Scene 3 lines 38–51

1 Re-read Feste's love song . What does he think love is? How does this contrast with Orsino's view of love in the opening scene of the play?
2 Sir Toby and Sir Andrew use slang and other words which are no longer used.
   • Make a glossary of slang words and expressions from this scene.
   • Explain what each word or phrase means, suggesting modern equivalents.

- Add to the glossary as you read more of the play.

Writing

1 Imagine that Antonio, returning to his room, finds a farewell letter from Sebastian. Write the letter he might leave.
2 Write Sebastian's diary entry in which he explains what he hopes to gain from his journey.
3 During the last part of Act 2 scene 3 Feste is presumably present and listening to Maria's plans to make a fool of Malvolio. Either
   - write a director's note on what an actor playing Feste should do, or
   - write a short piece explaining, from his point of view, what passes through his mind as he listens to her plans.
4 Imagine that Feste provides a humorous column for *Illyria Illustrated*. For the next edition his headline is 'Why I love me, or, 'I used to be conceited but now I'm perfect'. The article will apparently be by A. Steward. Write it.

Quiz

1 What was Viola's father's name?
2 Who is a churlish messenger?
3 What, according to Sir Andrew, does life consist of?
4 Who, according to Maria, believes that '*all that look on him love him*'?
5 Which two characters are compared, humorously, to dogs.

Orsino requests music to sooth his emotions but Feste is not available to sing the old song which he would prefer to hear. While he listens to instrumentalists playing the melody he asks Cesario whether he has ever experienced the pangs of love.

---

antic: quaint, old-fashioned

passion: (unrequited) love

light airs…times: the superficial melodies and contrived words which are the fashion of these changeable and fast-moving times

Unstaid…beloved: excitable and unstable in my emotions, though I keep my beloved constantly in my imagination

the seat…throned: i.e. the heart

favour: face

by your favour: with your permission – with a pun on the meaning in the previous line

Scene 4

The Duke's Palace
Enter DUKE, VIOLA *as* CESARIO, CURIO, *and others*

DUKE
Give me some music. Now, good morrow,
    friends.
Now, good Cesario, but that piece of song,
That old and antic song we heard last night;
Methought it did relieve my passion much,
More than light airs and recollected terms
Of these most brisk and giddy-paced times.
Come, but one verse.

CURIO
He is not here, so please your lordship, that should
sing it.

DUKE
Who was it?   10

CURIO
Feste, the jester, my lord; a fool that the lady
Olivia's father took much delight in. He is about
the house.

DUKE
Seek him out, and play the tune the while.
                      [Exit Curio. Music plays
Come hither, boy. If ever thou shalt love,
In the sweet pangs of it remember me;
For such as I am all true lovers are,
Unstaid and skittish in all motions else,
Save in the constant image of the creature
That is beloved. How dost thou like this tune?   20

VIOLA
It gives a very echo to the seat
Where love is throned.

DUKE
                      Thou dost speak masterly.
My life upon 't, young though thou art, thine eye
Hath stayed upon some favour that it loves;
Hath it not, boy?

VIOLA
                    A little, by your favour.

Cesario says that the person he loves is very similar to Orsino but Orsino tells him that in marriage the man should be the older partner. Feste enters and begins his song which is about the sadness of unrequited love.

---

so wears...level: she adapts herself to him and becomes a steadying influence on him

hold the bent: take the strain (like a bent bow)

spinsters: women who spin wool

free maids...bones: carefree lace makers

silly sooth: simple truth

dallies with: dwells on

the old age: the mythical Golden Age, characterized by plenty, simplicity, and gentle pleasures

prithee: please, from 'I pray thee'

cypress: wood used for coffins and hence a symbol of mourning

DUKE   What kind of woman is't?

VIOLA   Of your complexion.

DUKE   She is not worth thee then. What years, i' faith?

VIOLA   About your years, my lord.

DUKE   Too old, by heaven. Let still the woman take
       An elder than herself: so wears she to him,   30
       So sways she level in her husband's heart.
       For, boy, however we do praise ourselves,
       Our fancies are more giddy and unfirm,
       More longing, wavering, sooner lost and worn,
       Than women's are.

VIOLA   I think it well, my lord.

DUKE   Then let thy love be younger than thyself,
       Or thy affection cannot hold the bent;
       For women are as roses, whose fair flower
       Being once displayed, doth fall that very hour.

VIOLA   And so they are; alas, that they are so –   40
       To die, even when they to perfection grow.

       Enter CURIO *and* FESTE

DUKE   O fellow, come, the song we had last night.
       Mark it, Cesario, it is old and plain;
       The spinsters and the knitters in the sun,
       And the free maids that weave their threads with
          bones,
       Do use to chant it; it is silly sooth,
       And dallies with the innocence of love,
       Like the old age.

FESTE   Are you ready, sir?

DUKE   Ay, prithee sing.   [*Music* 50

FESTE   [*Sings*]
       Come away, come away, death,
          And in sad cypress let me be laid;
       Fie away, fie away, breath,
          I am slain by a fair cruel maid.

Feste concludes his song, is paid, wishes Orsino
satisfaction from his sadness and leaves. Orsino sends
Cesario back to Olivia with another message of love.

strown: scattered (past participle of 'strew')
paid: paid for
the melancholy god: i.e. Saturn, presiding god of the Golden
  Age but later associated with a cold and gloomy
  temperament
changeable taffeta: shot silk which, like opal, changes its
  colour according to the light
I would...nothing: Feste suggests that since inconstant men
  are like the sea, subject to changing moods and essentially
  directionless, they would make good sailors. They would be
  content with an aimless voyage.
sovereign cruelty: unkind queen of my heart
Prizes...lands: does not value material wealth
The parts: the qualities
giddily as fortune: mere good luck
that miracle...in: the beauty with which Nature has
  dressed her

My shroud of white, stuck all with yew,
> O prepare it.
My part of death no one so true
> Did share it.

Not a flower, not a flower sweet,
> On my black coffin let there be strown;   60
Not a friend, not a friend greet
> My poor corpse, where my bones shall be
> thrown.
A thousand thousand sighs to save,
> Lay me, O where
Sad true lover never find my grave,
> To weep there.

DUKE   [*Giving him money*] There's for thy pains.

FESTE   No pains, sir; I take pleasure in singing, sir.

DUKE   I'll pay thy pleasure then.

FESTE   Truly, sir, and pleasure will be paid, one time or   70
another.

DUKE   Give me now leave to leave thee.

FESTE   Now the melancholy god protect thee, and the
tailor make thy doublet of changeable taffeta, for
thy mind is a very opal. I would have men of such
constancy put to sea, that their business might be
everything and their intent everywhere; for that's it
that always makes a good voyage of nothing.
Farewell.   [*Exit*

DUKE   Let all the rest give place.

> [*Exeunt Curio and others*
> Once more, Cesario,   80
Get thee to yond same sovereign cruelty.
Tell her, my love, more noble than the world,
Prizes not quantity of dirty lands;
The parts that fortune hath bestowed upon her,
Tell her, I hold as giddily as fortune.
But 'tis that miracle and queen of gems

Orsino tells Cesario that it is not possible that Olivia will continue to reject him since men love more strongly than women. Cesario disagrees and says that her father's daughter (herself) loved patiently and silently, unable to express her love.

---

a pang of heart: a deep-seated painful emotion

There is no...heart: – the notion that women were not strong enough for the kind of passionate, intense love which men experienced was a common Elizabethan idea

retention: control, power (see Act 5 scene 1 line 78)

appetite: merely lust

No motion...revolt: not deeply felt emotion but merely infatuation which ultimately sickens (compare Act 1 scene 1 lines 1–3)

mine: i.e. my love

let concealment...cheek: kept her secret which, like a grub inside a rose bud, destroyed the healthy pink of her cheek

damask: pink, like the damask rose

melancholy: sadness, depression

Patience on a monument: this personification often occurred in memorial carvings

Our shows...will: we show outwardly more than we really feel

still we prove...love: we men always vow to love but fail to live up to our oaths

That nature pranks her in attracts my soul.

VIOLA   But if she cannot love you, sir?

DUKE   I cannot be so answered.

VIOLA   Sooth, but you must.
          Say that some lady, as perhaps there is,   90
          Hath for your love as great a pang of heart
          As you have for Olivia. You cannot love her;
          You tell her so. Must she not then be answered?

DUKE   There is no woman's sides
          Can bide the beating of so strong a passion
          As love doth give my heart; no woman's heart
          So big, to hold so much; they lack retention.
          Alas, their love may be called appetite,
          No motion of the liver, but the palate,
          That suffer surfeit, cloyment and revolt;   100
          But mine is all as hungry as the sea,
          And can digest as much. Make no compare
          Between that love a woman can bear me
          And that I owe Olivia.

VIOLA   Ay, but I know –

DUKE   What dost thou know?

VIOLA   Too well what love women to men may owe.
          In faith, they are as true of heart as we.
          My father had a daughter loved a man,
          As it might be perhaps, were I a woman,
          I should your lordship.

DUKE   And what's her history?   110

VIOLA   A blank, my lord. She never told her love,
          But let concealment, like a worm i' the bud,
          Feed on her damask cheek. She pined in thought,
          And with a green and yellow melancholy
          She sat like Patience on a monument,
          Smiling at grief. Was not this love indeed?
          We men may say more, swear more, but indeed
          Our shows are more than will; for still we prove

Cesario nearly gives her hidden identity away and makes a swift exit. She takes a present to Olivia from Orsino.

---

give no...denay: give way to no-one nor accept any denial

Fabian joins Sir Toby and Sir Andrew since he too has a grudge against Malvolio. Maria tells them to hide because Malvolio is coming down the path.

---

a scruple: the tiniest part

let me...melancholy: since melancholy was considered a cold humour Fabian is joking

niggardly: miserly

sheep-biter: literally, a dog that worries sheep, but the phrase was used metaphorically to describe sneaks and hypocrites. Here it also prepares for the reference to bear-baiting, an activity especially disapproved of by puritans.

he brought...with: turned Olivia against me

we will...blue: metaphorically, beat him black and blue with our jokes at his expense

metal of India: gold, thus metaphorically 'priceless' and with a pun on metal/mettle: high-spirited

contemplative idiot: deeply thoughtful fool

Much in our vows, but little in our love.

DUKE   But died thy sister of her love, my boy?   120

VIOLA   I am all the daughters of my father's house,
                  And all the brothers too – and yet I know not.
                  Sir, shall I to this lady?

DUKE   Ay, that's the theme.
                  To her in haste; give her this jewel; say,
                  My love can give no place, bide no denay.

                                                        [*Exeunt*

Scene 5

Olivia's House
Enter SIR TOBY, SIR ANDREW, *and* FABIAN

SIR TOBY   Come thy ways, Signior Fabian.

FABIAN   Nay, I'll come; if I lose a scruple of this sport, let me
                  be boiled to death with melancholy.

SIR TOBY   Wouldst thou not be glad to have the niggardly
                  rascally sheep-biter come by some notable shame?

FABIAN   I would exult, man. You know he brought me out
                  o' favour with my lady about a bear-baiting here.

SIR TOBY   To anger him we'll have the bear again; and we will
                  fool him black and blue, shall we not, Sir Andrew?

SIR ANDREW   An we do not, it is pity of our lives.   10

                  Enter MARIA

SIR TOBY   Here comes the little villain. How now, my metal of
                  India!

MARIA   Get ye all three into the box-tree. Malvolio's
                  coming down this walk; he has been yonder i' the
                  sun practising behaviour to his own shadow this half
                  hour. Observe him, for the love of mockery; for I
                  know this letter will make a contemplative idiot of

Maria drops a letter on the path. Malvolio is talking to himself and imagining his marriage to Olivia, much to the disgust of the two knights.

Close: hide
trout...tickling: proverbially, to trap someone by flattery
she did affect me: i.e. Olivia admired me
uses: treats
overweening: arrogant, ambitious
Contemplation: thoughts, day-dreams
turkey-cock...plumes: the strutting ('*jets*') and raised feathers ('*advanced plumes*') of the bird were a common metaphor of self-importance
'Slight: by God's light
Pistol him: shoot him with a pistol
the lady...wardrobe: possibly a topical reference but the allusion has never been explained
Jezebel: the arrogant widow of King Ahab (Old Testament, Book of Kings) who paid for her behaviour by being thrown to her death and eaten by dogs
blows-him: inflates him with pride
stone-bow: crossbow or catapult which would fire a small stone
branched: embroidered with designs of foliage
Fire and brimstone!: Hell! Fire and brimstone (sulphur) being traditionally associated with the devil.

him. Close, in the name of jesting. Lie thou there
[*throws down a letter*]; for here comes the trout that
must be caught with tickling.   20

[*Exit*

Enter MALVOLIO

MALVOLIO   'Tis but fortune; all is fortune. Maria once told me
she did affect me; and I have heard herself come
thus near that, should she fancy, it should be one of
my complexion. Besides she uses me with a more
exalted respect than any one else that follows her.
What should I think on't?

SIR TOBY   Here's an overweening rogue.

FABIAN   O peace! Contemplation makes a rare turkey-cock
of him; how he jets under his advanced plumes.

SIR ANDREW 'Slight, I could so beat the rogue!   30

SIR TOBY   Peace, I say.

MALVOLIO   To be Count Malvolio.

SIR TOBY   Ah, rogue!

SIR ANDREW Pistol him, pistol him.

SIR TOBY   Peace, peace.

MALVOLIO   There is example for't; the lady of the Strachy
married the yeoman of the wardrobe.

SIR ANDREW Fie on him, Jezebel!

FABIAN   O, peace. Now he's deeply in; look how
imagination blows him.   40

MALVOLIO   Having been three months married to her, sitting in
my state –

SIR TOBY   O for a stone-bow to hit him in the eye.

MALVOLIO   Calling my officers about me, in my branched velvet
gown; having come from a day-bed, where I have
left Olivia sleeping –

SIR TOBY   Fire and brimstone!

Malvolio imagines himself telling Sir Toby what to do and how to behave. He comments on Sir Andrew's foolishness and then sees the letter on the path.

to have…regard: enjoying my authority I gravely survey those around me

Bolts and shackles: fetters, to chain Malvolio in prison

play…jewel: he almost forgets that he will no longer be wearing his steward's chain of office

courtesies: bows, makes a courtesy or curtsy

cars: carts – the metaphor is of torture by being torn apart between two carts. Fabian continues it at line 72.

an austere…control: a severe, controlling look

give me…speech: allow me the right to speak to you

break the sinew: ruin, disable

the woodcock…gin: the bird is near the trap (woodcocks being proverbially stupid)

the spirit…intimate: may he be inspired by the spirit which governs his behaviour (to read the letter aloud)

FABIAN	O, peace, peace.
MALVOLIO	And then to have the humour of state; and after a
	demure travel of regard, telling them I know 50
	my place as I would they should do theirs, to ask for
	my kinsman Toby –
SIR TOBY	Bolts and shackles!
FABIAN	O peace, peace, peace. Now, now.
MALVOLIO	Seven of my people with an obedient start make out
	for him. I frown the while, and perchance wind up
	my watch, or play with my – some rich jewel. Toby
	approaches; courtesies there to me –
SIR TOBY	Shall this fellow live?
FABIAN	Though our silence be drawn from us with cars, 60
	yet peace.
MALVOLIO	I extend my hand to him thus, quenching my
	familiar smile with an austere regard of control –
SIR TOBY	And does not Toby take you a blow o' the lips
	then?
MALVOLIO	Saying, 'Cousin Toby, my fortunes having cast me
	on your niece give me this prerogative of
	speech' –
SIR TOBY	What, what?
MALVOLIO	'You must amend your drunkenness.' 70
SIR TOBY	Out, scab!
FABIAN	Nay, patience, or we break the sinew of our plot.
MALVOLIO	'Besides, you waste the treasure of your time with a
	foolish knight' –
SIR ANDREW	That's me, I warrant you.
MALVOLIO	'One Sir Andrew' –
SIR ANDREW	I knew 'twas I, for many do call me fool.
MALVOLIO	[*Seeing the letter*] What employment have we here?
FABIAN	Now is the woodcock near the gin.
SIR TOBY	O, peace. And the spirit of humours intimate 80

He picks up the letter and thinks he recognizes Olivia's handwriting and her seal. He opens it and reads a love poem full of cryptic clues about the beloved which he thinks refer to him.

her very C's...P's: 'C' and 'P' do not occur in '*To the unknown beloved, this, and my good wishes*', which is the superscription of the letter but they allow for two vulgar jokes (see Act 2 scene 3 line 182 and note)

in contempt of question: without doubt

the impressure her Lucrece: the letter has been sealed with wax into which Olivia's seal has been pressed. This has an engraving of Lucrece, considered a symbol of female honour since she killed herself after being raped by Tarquin. Shakespeare told the story in a narrative poem.

liver and all: his emotions as well as the rest of him (see Act 1 scene 1 line 37 and Act 2 scene 4 line 99)

numbers: metre

brock: badger, poverbially smelly

fustian: pointless, worthless; from fustian cloth which was heavy but cheap. Fabian's comment tells us that there is no point in looking for some subtle meaning in the letter.

the staniel checks at it: the kestrel turns, distracted by it reading aloud to him.

MALVOLIO   [*Taking up the letter*] By my life, this is my lady's hand: these be her very C's, her U's and her T's, and thus makes she her great P's. It is in contempt of question her hand.

SIR ANDREW   Her C's, her U's, and her T's. Why that –

MALVOLIO   [*Reads*] 'To the unknown beloved, this, and my good wishes.' Her very phrases. By your leave, wax. Soft – and the impressure her Lucrece, with which she uses to seal. 'Tis my lady. To whom should   90
this be?

FABIAN   This wins him, liver and all.

MALVOLIO   [*Reads*]
    'Jove knows I love,
      But who?
    Lips do not move;
    No man must know.'
'No man must know.' What follows? The numbers altered. 'No man must know.' If this should be thee, Malvolio?

SIR TOBY   Marry, hang thee, brock!   100

MALVOLIO   [*Reads*]
    'I may command where I adore;
      But silence, like a Lucrece knife,
    With bloodless stroke my heart doth gore;
      M. O. A. I. doth sway my life.'

FABIAN   A fustian riddle.

SIR TOBY   Excellent wench, say I.

MALVOLIO   'M. O. A. I. doth sway my life.' Nay, but first, let me see, let me see, let me see.

FABIAN   What dish o' poison has she dressed him!

SIR TOBY   And with what wing the staniel checks at it!   110

MALVOLIO   'I may command where I adore.' Why, she may

Having convinced himself, on the basis of very thin evidence, that the poem shows that Olivia loves him, Malvolio reads the letter. This appears to instruct him to be bold, proud, argumentative with Sir Toby and wear yellow stockings...

---

formal capacity: sensible and aware person

what should...portend: what is the significance of those letters placed in that order

M. O. A. I.: these letters all appear in Malvolio's name, but not in this order. Some scholars have searched for other significance in them but this is to make the same mistake as Malvolio. Sir Toby puns on two of the letters – '*O, ay*' – and comments that Malvolio is on a hopeless quest, '*a cold scent*'.

Sowter: cobbler; metaphorically, a bungler. Also a common name for a hunting dog.

cur: mongrel dog, referring back to Fabian's previous speech

there is...probation: the following letters are not in the right order; they don't bear probing

O shall end: omega, the last letter of the Greek alphabet, with a pun on the O of the hangman's noose

detraction at your heels: misfortunes to come, the detractors hiding in the box tree

simulation: puzzle

to crush...bow to me: if I mangled the letters a little they would point in my direction

revolve: consider

inure: accustom

slough: (pronounced 'sluff') skin, especially of a snake – metaphorically, clothes and bearing

tang: clang like a bell

put thyself...singularity: behave in an eccentric, individual manner

yellow stockings: suitable for a fun-loving young man. Yellow is a symbol of jealousy.

	command me: I serve her; she is my lady. Why, this is evident to any formal capacity; there is no obstruction in this. And the end – what should that alphabetical position portend? If I could make that resemble something in me, Softly – M. O. A. I.
SIR TOBY	O, ay, make up that; he is now at a cold scent.
FABIAN	Sowter will cry upon't for all this, though it be as rank as a fox.
MALVOLIO	M – Malvolio – M – why, that begins my name. 120
FABIAN	Did I not say he would work it out? The cur is excellent at faults.
MALVOLIO	M – but then there is no consonancy in the sequel, that suffers under probation: A should follow, but O does.
FABIAN	And O shall end, I hope.
SIR TOBY	Ay, or I'll cudgel him, and make him cry 'O!'
MALVOLIO	And then I comes behind.
FABIAN	Ay, an you had any eye behind you, you might see more detraction at your heels than fortunes 130 before you.
MALVOLIO	M. O. A. I. This simulation is not as the former; and yet to crush this a little, it would bow to me, for every one of these letters are in my name. Soft, here follows prose. [*Reads*] 'If this fall into thy hand, revolve. In my stars I am above thee; but be not afraid of greatness. Some are born great, some achieve greatness and some have greatness thrust upon 'em. Thy Fates open their hands, let thy blood and spirit embrace them; and to inure 140 thyself to what thou art like to be, cast thy humble slough and appear fresh. Be opposite with a kinsman, surly with servants; let thy tongue tang arguments of state; put thyself into the trick of singularity. She thus advises thee that sighs for thee. Remember who commended thy yellow stockings,

...which should be held up with crossed garters. Malvolio decides to follow the instructions exactly. He reads the ps which tells him to smile constantly, and exits to put his plan into action. The conspirators come out of hiding and Sir Toby is so delighted with the success of the plot that he says he could marry Maria out of gratitude for it.

---

cross-gartered: garters which crossed the leg both above and below the knee; another youthful fashion

Go to: come on!

fellow: associate

champaign: open countryside

politic authors: books about government and statecraft

I will wash...acquaintance: I will avoid common people, as I would wash away dirt

point-device...man: exactly the man described in the letter

jade: make an idiot of

injunction: command

strange, stout: distant, arrogant

even with...putting on: as quickly as I can

entertainest: accept

Sophy: the Shah. The reference is probably topical, suggested by news, published in 1600, of the visit of Sir Anthony Shirley to the Persian court. The Sophy was rumoured to be fabulously wealthy.

and wished to see thee ever cross-gartered. I say,
remember. Go to, thou art made, if thou desirest to
be so. If not, let me see thee a steward still, the
fellow of servants, and not worthy to touch   150
Fortune's fingers. Farewell. She that would
alter services with thee,

    THE FORTUNATE-UNHAPPY.'

Daylight and champaign discovers not more. This is
open. I will be proud, I will read politic authors, I
will baffle Sir Toby, I will wash off gross
acquaintance, I will be point-device the very man. I
do not now fool myself to let imagination jade me;
for every reason excites to this, that my lady loves
me. She did commend my yellow stockings of   160
late, she did praise my leg being cross-gartered; and
in this she manifests herself to my love, and with a
kind of injunction drives me to these habits of her
liking. I thank my stars I am happy. I will be
strange, stout, in yellow stockings, and cross-
gartered, even with the swiftness of putting on. Jove
and my stars be praised. Here is yet a postscript.
[*Reads*] 'Thou canst not choose but know who I
am. If thou entertainest my love, let it appear in thy
smiling; thy smiles become thee well. Therefore   170
in my presence still smile, dear my sweet, I
prithee.' Jove, I thank thee. I will smile, I will do
everything that thou wilt have me.

                               [*Exit*

FABIAN	I will not give my part of this sport for a pension of thousands to be paid from the Sophy.
SIR TOBY	I could marry this wench for this device.
SIR ANDREW	So could I too.
SIR TOBY	And ask no other dowry with her but such another jest.
SIR ANDREW	Nor I neither. 180

Enter MARIA

Maria enters to discover whether Malvolio has fallen for
the plot. Sir Toby, swearing to be her slave, tells her that
the trick will drive Malvolio mad. Maria tells them that
Malvolio's changed behaviour will offend Olivia and they
all go off to see what will happen.

gull-catcher: trickster, one who catches out a fool
play...tray-trip: wager my freedom on the chance of throwing
    threes in a dice game
thy bond-slave: thy property by signing a contract
thou hast put...mad: you have plunged him into a fantasy
    world so that when he emerges from it and sees what has
    happened to him he will go mad
aqua-vitae: brandy, whisky or other strong spirits which the
    midwife might use to relieve her stress or that of her patient
fruits: result
it cannot...contempt: it is bound to ruin his reputation
Tartar: Tartarus; hell in classical mythology
I'll make one too: I'll join you

ACTIVITIES

Keeping track

Scene 4

1 Why does Orsino send for Feste?
2 What does Viola/Cesario tell Orsino about the woman
    she/he loves?
3 What advice does Orsino give Cesario about the woman 'he'
    should love?

FABIAN	Here comes my noble gull-catcher.
SIR TOBY	Wilt thou set thy foot o' my neck?
SIR ANDREW	Or o' mine either?
SIR TOBY	Shall I play my freedom at tray-trip, and become thy bond-slave?
SIR ANDREW	I' faith, or I either?
SIR TOBY	Why, thou hast put him in such a dream, that when the image of it leaves him he must run mad.
MARIA	Nay, but say true; does it work upon him?
SIR TOBY	Like aqua-vitae with a midwife. 190
MARIA	If you will then see the fruits of the sport, mark his first approach before my lady. He will come to her in yellow stockings, and 'tis a colour she abhors, and cross-gartered, a fashion she detests; and he will smile upon her, which will now be so unsuitable to her disposition, being addicted to a melancholy as she is, that it cannot but turn him into a notable contempt. If you will see it, follow me.
SIR TOBY	To the gates of Tartar, thou most excellent devil of wit. 200
SIR ANDREW	I'll make one too.

[Exeunt

---

4 In his song and conversation with Orsino how does Feste describe the behaviour of a lover?
5 What issue do Orsino and Cesario debate and disagree on?
6 What does Cesario say about 'his' sister's love?
7 What is Cesario really describing?

Scene 5

8 Why does Fabian join the conspiracy to take revenge on Malvolio?

9 Where do the conspirators hide?

10 Malvolio thinks that he is on his own. What is he dreaming about?

11 What, according to the letter, must Malvolio do in order to demonstrate his love for Olivia?

12 How does Sir Toby react to the trick and how does he feel about Maria as a result of it?

Discussion

1 After the merriment and light-heartedness of scene 3, how would you describe the mood of scene 4?

2 'Duke Orsino enjoys being sad and feeling sorry for himself; he does not actually do very much to win Olivia's love or respect.' How far would you agree with this judgement? Find evidence in scene 4 to support your argument.

3 Orsino often comments on the differences between men and women, especially in their emotions.
   • Do you think that such differences exist?
   • If you do, what are they and why do they exist? (Is it because men are different from women or is it because society expects different forms of behaviour from each sex?)

4 Viola is very attracted to Orsino.
   • How does she describe her love for him without giving her true identity away?
   • Does Orsino suspect anything?

5 Do you feel any sense of pity for Malvolio?

Drama

Heartbroken

• Work in groups of four or five.
• Re-read Feste's melancholy song (scene 4 lines 51–66).
• One member of your group should become Feste; the rest become the Duke, Cesario and other courtiers.
• Feste reads the song slowly and with maximum emotion in order to please the Duke.

- The characters should react in appropriate ways. They may not all be able to treat it with equal seriousness.

Friendly advice

Viola has no-one to confide in, yet she must be very confused.
- Work in groups of three.
- Imagine you are Viola's friends. You know that she is in disguise. Plan what advice you would give her.
- One person from each group should then adopt the role of Viola.
- The Violas should each go to another group and receive the advice that has been prepared. How does Viola respond?

Hidden watchers

Act 2 scene 5 is very funny. Much humour comes from the steady development as one comic situation follows swiftly on from another. To appreciate this, perform the whole scene.
- Work in groups of five or six.
- One person reads Malvolio's lines and plans his moves.
- The others in the group become the four hidden watchers. Read their lines to work out their moves and gestures.
- Decide what to use to represent the tree. A small object such as a chair could increase the humour.
- Does Malvolio hear or see anything?
- Perform the scene, complete with Malvolio's lines and the watchers' moves.
- Try to keep it moving briskly.

Characters

Orsino

1 Some people are very irritated by Orsino's behaviour and attitude. For example, they say that he is sentimental, selfish and boastful. Look closely at scene 4, starting with Feste's comments about Orsino (lines 73–78), and find what evidence you can to support these criticisms.

Viola

2 Viola shows her intelligence and wit in several ways in scene 4. She tells the Duke about her love for him but does not give her true identity away. How does she do this?

Malvolio

3 Look at Malvolio's speeches before he picks up the letter.
  • Describe in detail what he is talking about.
  • In what ways is he ready to be deceived by the letter?
  • Compare Malvolio's behaviour in this scene (when he thinks he is alone) with the way in which he has behaved in public previously. What differences are there? Is he a hypocrite?

Maria

4 Maria is a clever woman. How is this revealed in the letter?

Close study

Scene 4 lines 15–41 and 80–125

1 Re-read Viola's conversations with the Duke. What attitudes to women does Orsino show in this scene? Refer as closely as possible to particular phrases and the imagery he chooses to use. What does this tell us about his character?

Scene 4 lines 51–66

2 Re-read Feste's song '*Come away, come away, death*'.
  • Do you think people really die from love?
  • Is the song, or the story it tells, supposed to be taken seriously?
  • From whose point of view is this song written?
  • What effect does it have within this scene?
  • Why does it seem to be of particular interest to Orsino?

Scene 4 lines 111–119

3 Look at Viola's speech which begins '*She never told her love...*' Put the speech in your own words, explaining Shakespeare's metaphorical language.

Writing

1 Interview Orsino about his lifestyle and his ideas about women and love.
   • Write the article for *Illyria Illustrated*.
2 Imagine Feste writes about the evening and day he has spent in Orsino's house. What does he say about the Duke's behaviour and character?
3 Orsino writes anonymously to the agony column of *Illyria Illustrated*. Write his letter and the reply he receives which gives him advice or solace with regard to his love for Olivia. Try the same exercise for Malvolio, Viola and Sir Andrew.
4 Orsino seems fascinated by Cesario at this point in the play. Write a diary entry from his point of view about his feelings for Cesario, including a list of questions that he might want to ask 'him' bearing in mind the information that Viola has given him about herself.
5 Compose the poem that Viola might write about her love for Orsino.
6 Write a story in which somebody has persuaded you that the most gorgeous girl or boy in school is madly in love with you and wants to go out with you. Describe how you feel and what preparations you make for the date. What happens?

Quiz

Who:
1 was not available when required
2 spoke masterly
3 thinks a man should marry a woman younger than himself
4 is paid
5 never told her love
6 thinks she is all her father's children (but isn't)
7 is in the box tree
8 is a turkey-cock, a woodcock and a badger
9 could marry Maria
10 is addicted to melancholy?

Cesario meets Feste. They play with words and Feste comments on the difficulty in understanding words or using them with precision and honesty.

1 Viola, meeting Feste for the first time, asks him if he earns his money as a musician, accompanying himself on a side drum. In reply Feste plays on the phrase '*live by*'. Viola continues the word game.

2 Feste concludes that words can be very easily turned inside out. They don't necessarily mean what was originally intended.

3 As an example he suggests that his sister could gain a 'bad' name through the use or misuse of it by others.

Act three

Scene 1

Olivia's Garden
Enter VIOLA *as* CESARIO, *and* FESTE *playing on pipe and tabor*

VIOLA	Save thee, friend, and thy music. Dost thou live by thy tabor?
FESTE	No, sir, I live by the church.
VIOLA	Art thou a churchman?
FESTE	No such matter, sir: I do live by the church; for I do live at my house, and my house doth stand by the church.
VIOLA	So thou mayst say the king lies by a beggar, if a beggar dwell near him; or the church stands by thy tabor, if thy tabor stand by the church. 10
FESTE	You have said, sir. To see this age! A sentence is but a cheveril glove to a good wit: how quickly the wrong side may be turned outward.
VIOLA	Nay, that's certain; they that dally nicely with words may quickly make them wanton.
FESTE	I would, therefore, my sister had had no name, sir.
VIOLA	Why, man?
FESTE	Why, sir, her name's a word, and to dally with that word might make my sister wanton. But indeed, words are very rascals since bonds disgraced 20 them.
VIOLA	The reason, man?
FESTE	Troth, sir, I can yield you none without words, and words are grown so false I am loath to prove reason with them.

The exchange of wit continues with Feste commenting on the folly of marriage. Cesario gives him coins and Feste offers to tell Olivia of his arrival.

her corrupter of words: her maker of word-plays, but Feste is referring back to his earlier comments to Viola about the untrustworthiness of words and those who use them

the orb: the Earth

the fool: Feste refers both to himself and to foolishness in general

your wisdom: your foolishness; Feste is ironic

my chin: with the accent on '*my*'

these: i.e. the coin

Lord Pandarus...a beggar: in a legend of the Trojan Wars Pandarus arranged meetings between his niece, Cressida, and her lover, Prince Troilus. The affair ended tragically and in one version of the story Cressida died a beggar.

The matter...beggar: since you ask a beggar to help you I hope that your mission is unimportant

conster: explain

VIOLA	I warrant thou art a merry fellow and carest for nothing.
FESTE	Not so, sir, I do care for something; but in my conscience, sir, I do not care for you. If that be to care for nothing, sir, I would it would make you invisible. 30
VIOLA	Art not thou the Lady Olivia's fool?
FESTE	No indeed, sir, the Lady Olivia has no folly; she will keep no fool, sir, till she be married; and fools are as like husbands as pilchards are to herrings – the husband's the bigger. I am indeed not her fool, but her corrupter of words.
VIOLA	I saw thee late at the Count Orsino's.
FESTE	Foolery, sir, does walk about the orb like the sun, it shines everywhere. I would be sorry, sir, but the fool should be as oft with your master as with my mistress: I think I saw your wisdom there. 40
VIOLA	Nay, an thou pass upon me, I'll no more with thee. Hold, there's expenses for thee. [Gives him a coin]
FESTE	Now Jove in his next commodity of hair send thee a beard.
VIOLA	By my troth, I'll tell thee, I am almost sick for one; [Aside] though I would not have it grow on my chin. Is thy lady within?
FESTE	Would not a pair of these have bred, sir? 50
VIOLA	Yes, being kept together and put to use.
FESTE	I would play Lord Pandarus of Phrygia, sir, to bring a Cressida to this Troilus.
VIOLA	I understand you, sir; 'tis well begged. [Gives him another coin]
FESTE	The matter, I hope, is not great, sir, begging but a beggar: Cressida was a beggar. My lady is within, sir. I will conster to them whence you come; who you

Viola comments on the wisdom shown by the fool who is a precise observer of human behaviour. Reverting to her role as Cesario she is met by Sir Toby who is sarcastically courteous. Olivia and Maria appear.

welkin: element. Both words could mean 'sky'; in changing the appropriate word for an inappropriate synonym Feste is proving how '*words are grown so false*'

craves...wit: demands some sort of intelligence

their mood...jests: the mood of those people who are the butt of his jokes

quality: social status

haggard...feather: wild hawk which attacks at every opportunity

a practice...art: this profession (of jesting) is as difficult as any intellectual work

For folly...their wit: the fool's well-directed fooling is appropriate – men who think themselves wise but act foolishly merely show themselves up

4 Sir Toby and Sir Andrew now demonstrate the truth of Viola's words in the sarcastic, over-exaggerated politeness of their greeting.

5 Viola greets Olivia in courtly language which Sir Andrew immediately attempts to learn by heart.

are and what you would are out of my welkin – I
might say 'element', but the word is over-worn.

[Exit

VIOLA   This fellow is wise enough to play the fool,   60
And to do that well craves a kind of wit.
He must observe their mood on whom he jests,
The quality of persons, and the time;
And, like the haggard, check at every feather
That comes before his eye. This is a practice
As full of labour as a wise man's art;
For folly that he wisely shows is fit,
But wise men, folly-fall'n, quite taint their wit.

Enter SIR TOBY *and* SIR ANDREW

SIR TOBY   Save you, gentleman.

VIOLA   And you, sir.   70

SIR ANDREW   Dieu vous garde, monsieur.

VIOLA   Et vous aussi, votre serviteur.

SIR ANDREW   I hope, sir, you are; and I am yours.

SIR TOBY   Will you encounter the house? My niece is desirous
you should enter, if your trade be to her.

VIOLA   I am bound to your niece, sir; I mean she is the list
of my voyage.

SIR TOBY   Taste your legs, sir, put them to motion.

VIOLA   My legs do better understand me, sir, than I
understand what you mean by bidding me taste   80
my legs.

SIR TOBY   I mean, to go, sir, to enter.

VIOLA   I will answer you with gait and entrance. But we are
prevented.

Enter OLIVIA *and* MARIA

Most excellent accomplished lady, the heavens rain
odours on you.

SIR ANDREW   That youth's a rare courtier: 'Rain odours' – well.

**Olivia speaks with Cesario alone. She wishes to hear
nothing about Orsino but confesses she used the device of
the ring to ensure that Cesario would return.**

---

6 Olivia firmly dismisses her unwanted company.   6

Since...compliment: since pretended humility was thought
  complimentary
Would they were blanks: I wish they were empty
whet your...behalf: sharpen your appetite for him
undertake another suit: plead on someone else's behalf
music from the spheres: perfect heavenly music
Give me...you: allow me, please
After the last...here: after you bewitched me on your previous
  visit
abuse: deceive
Under...sit: I must endure your harsh judgement
that: i.e. the ring
at the stake: like a bear being baited; see also next line and Act
  1 scene 3 line 89

VIOLA	My matter hath no voice, lady, but to your own most pregnant and vouchsafed ear.
SIR ANDREW	'Odours', 'pregnant' and 'vouchsafed' – I'll get 90 'em all three all ready.
OLIVIA	Let the garden door be shut, and leave me to my hearing. [*Exeunt Sir Toby, Sir Andrew, and Maria*] Give me your hand, sir.
VIOLA	My duty, madam, and most humble service.
OLIVIA	What is your name?
VIOLA	Cesario is your servant's name, fair princess.
OLIVIA	My servant, sir? 'Twas never merry world Since lowly feigning was called compliment You're servant to the Count Orsino, youth. 100
VIOLA	And he is yours, and his must needs be yours: Your servant's servant is your servant, madam.
OLIVIA	For him, I think not on him; for his thoughts, Would they were blanks rather than filled with me.
VIOLA	Madam, I come to whet your gentle thoughts On his behalf.
OLIVIA	O, by your leave, I pray you. I bade you never speak again of him; But would you undertake another suit, I had rather hear you to solicit that Than music from the spheres.
VIOLA	Dear lady – 110
OLIVIA	Give me leave, beseech you. I did send, After the last enchantment you did here, A ring in chase of you. So did I abuse Myself, my servant, and, I fear me, you. Under your hard construction must I sit, To force that on you in a shameful cunning Which you knew none of yours. What might you think? Have you not set mine honour at the stake,

Olivia reveals her passion for Cesario. Cesario pities but rejects her. Olivia accepts the impossibility of their love. Both agree that they are not what they seem to be. Olivia recognizes that Cesario is in love with someone else.

---

baited...think: in this metaphor, taken from bear-baiting, Olivia suggests that Viola/Cesario must think of her as declaring her love too openly

receiving: understanding, awareness

cypress: black gauze, a veil used during mourning

degree, grize: step

a vulgar proof: common experience

Why...again: if my love is hopeless then I may as well make the best of things

O world...wolf: if I am to be rejected I would rather it were by an honourable man like you than by someone who has exploited me

upbraids: reproaches

when wit...proper man: when you are old enough to marry your wife is likely to find she has a fine man. (The metaphor is ironic given the triple identity of the actor playing Viola.)

west...'Westward-ho!': they refer both to the opportunities presented to the young man who will go west to the New World and to the cry of the Thames boatmen who offered a journey upstream from the city to the court at Westminster

Grace and good disposition: may God grant you His blessing and a settled mind

You'll nothing: you have no message to send?

you do think...you are: you think you are in love when you are not; you do not behave as a lady of your rank should

your fool: the butt of your joke and your entertainment

A murderous guilt...hid: 'murder will out', but no more quickly than concealed love

        And baited it with all th' unmuzzled thoughts
        That tyrannous heart can think? To one of your
            receiving   120
        Enough is shown; a cypress, not a bosom,
        Hides my heart. So, let me hear you speak.

VIOLA   I pity you.

OLIVIA   That's a degree to love.

VIOLA   No, not a grize; for 'tis a vulgar proof
        That very oft we pity enemies.

OLIVIA   Why, then, methinks 'tis time to smile again.
        O world, how apt the poor are to be proud.
        If one should be a prey, how much the better
        To fall before the lion than the wolf.   [*Clock strikes*
        The clock upbraids me with the waste of time.   130
        Be not afraid, good youth, I will not have you;
        And yet, when wit and youth is come to harvest,
        Your wife is like to reap a proper man.
        There lies your way, due west.

VIOLA   Then 'Westward-ho!'
        Grace and good disposition attend your ladyship.
        You'll nothing, madam, to my lord by me?

OLIVIA   Stay.
        I prithee tell me what thou think'st of me.

VIOLA   That you do think you are not what you are.   140

OLIVIA   If I think so, I think the same of you.

VIOLA   Then think you right: I am not what I am.

OLIVIA   I would you were as I would have you be.

VIOLA   Would it be better, madam, than I am?
        I wish it might, for now I am your fool.

OLIVIA   [*Aside*] O, what a deal of scorn looks beautiful
        In the contempt and anger of his lip.
        A murderous guilt shows not itself more soon
        Than love that would seem hid. Love's night is
            noon;

Olivia states her love for Cesario even more openly but Cesario declares that he can never love a woman. Olivia invites him to see her again to press Orsino's case.

maugre: despite

Nor wit nor: neither wit nor

Do not extort…clause: do not use the fact that I am wooing you as a reason for your not loving me

For that…cause: it is not your fault that I woo you

reason…fetter: let this argument defeat your logic

deplore: sadly describe

for thou…love: you may possibly persuade the heart that now utterly rejects Orsino's love to accept it

Sir Andrew tells Sir Toby that he will go home since Olivia clearly likes Cesario more than she does him.

dear venom: Sir Toby indicates that Sir Andrew has been speaking angrily, like a snake spitting. The conversation must seem to have started before they arrive on stage.

yield: give

argument: evidence

[*To Viola*] Cesario, by the roses of the spring,   150
By maidhood, honour, truth and everything,
I love thee so that, maugre all thy pride,
Nor wit nor reason can my passion hide.
Do not extort thy reasons from this clause,
For that I woo, thou therefore hast no cause;
But rather reason thus with reason fetter:
Love sought is good, but given unsought is better.

VIOLA   By innocence I swear, and by my youth,
I have one heart, one bosom, and one truth,
And that no woman has, nor never none   160
Shall mistress be of it, save I alone.
And so adieu, good madam; never more
Will I my master's tears to you deplore.

OLIVIA   Yet come again; for thou perhaps mayst move
That heart, which now abhors, to like his love.

[*Exeunt*

Scene ②

Olivia's House
Enter SIR TOBY, SIR ANDREW, *and* FABIAN

SIR ANDREW No, faith, I'll not stay a jot longer.

SIR TOBY   Thy reason, dear venom, give thy reason.

FABIAN   You must needs yield your reason, Sir Andrew.

SIR ANDREW Marry, I saw your niece do more favours to the
            Count's serving-man than ever she bestowed upon
            me; I saw't i' the orchard.

SIR TOBY   Did she see thee the while, old boy? Tell me that.

SIR ANDREW As plain as I see you now.

FABIAN   This was a great argument of love in her toward
            you.   10

SIR ANDREW 'Slight, will you make an ass o' me?

Fabian suggests that Olivia was only trying to rouse Sir
Andrew's jealousy in the hope that he would make
advances towards her. Sir Andrew agrees to challenge
Cesario to a duel.

---

grand-jurymen: who decided whether the evidence was
   sufficient for a case to go to court
dormouse valour: sleeping courage, but also an oxymoron
   (see GLOSSARY page 236) which tilts at Sir Andrew's timidity
brimstone: sulphur, and as such often associated with fire and,
   consequently, hell (see Act 2 scene 5 line 47). It also
   described certain medicines.
accosted: (see Act 1 scene 3 line 47 etc.)
fire-new from the mint: like a coin freshly minted
balked: an opportunity wasted
double...this: doubly golden, i.e. like an article twice plated
   with gold (and a back-reference to mint)
Dutchman's: an allusion to William Barentz who died during a
   courageous voyage into the Arctic Circle in 1596–97
some laudable...policy: some praiseworthy fight or scheme
An't be: if it is to be
policy: scheming
Brownist: Puritan, a follower of Robert Browne
Challenge me: challenge ('*me*' gives added emphasis, as with
   '*build me*' in the previous line)
love-broker: match-maker
man's commendation...woman: a man's reputation with a
   woman
martial hand: war-like handwriting, perhaps bold and careless
curst: fierce
invention: arguments, fictions
licence of ink: the freedom that comes from writing a letter
   (when the person is not addressed face to face)
thou'st: insult him by addressing him in the familiar form
   'thou' instead of the correctly formal 'you'
bed of Ware: a famous wooden bedstead, over three metres
   square, which could sleep up to twelve people
gall: bitterness; oak galls were an ingredient of ink
goose-pen: with a goose quill, but goose could also mean fool
   and coward

FABIAN   I will prove it legitimate, sir, upon the oaths of
            judgement and reason.

SIR TOBY   And they have been grand-jurymen since before
            Noah was a sailor.

FABIAN   She did show favour to the youth in your sight only
            to exasperate you, to awake your dormouse valour,
            to put fire in your heart and brimstone in your liver.
            You should then have accosted her, and with some
            excellent jests, fire-new from the mint, you   20
            should have banged the youth into dumbness. This
            was looked for at your hand, and this was balked.
            The double gilt of this opportunity you let time
            wash off, and you are now sailed into the north of
            my lady's opinion, where you will hang like an icicle
            on a Dutchman's beard, unless you do redeem it by
            some laudable attempt either of valour or policy.

SIR ANDREW An't be any way, it must be with valour, for policy I
            hate. I had as lief be a Brownist as a politician.

SIR TOBY   Why, then, build me thy fortunes upon the basis   30
            of valour. Challenge me the Count's youth to fight
            with him; hurt him in eleven places. My niece shall
            take note of it; and assure thyself, there is no love-
            broker in the world can more prevail in man's
            commendation with woman than report of valour.

FABIAN   There is no way but this, Sir Andrew.

SIR ANDREW Will either of you bear me a challenge to him?

SIR TOBY   Go, write it in a martial hand; be curst and brief; it
            is no mater how witty, so it be eloquent and full of
            invention. Taunt him with the licence of ink. If   40
            thou thou'st him some thrice, it shall not be amiss;
            and as many lies as will lie in thy sheet of paper,
            although the sheet were big enough for the bed of
            Ware in England, set 'em down. Go, about it. Let
            there be gall enough in thy ink, though thou write
            with a goose-pen, no matter. About it.

SIR ANDREW Where shall I find you?

Sir Andrew goes off to write his challenge and Sir Toby
boasts of the money he has tricked from him. He agrees
with Fabian that neither Sir Andrew nor Cesario looks at
all belligerent. Maria enters to announce that Malvolio has
adopted the dress and behaviour required of him in her
letter.

---

cubiculo: small chamber

dear, dear: sweet, expensive

manikin: puppet, little man

some two thousand: roughly two thousand ducats (see Act 1
scene 3 line 21)

wainropes; hale: waggon ropes; pull forcibly

liver: believed to be the source of blood and thus of courage

th' anatomy: the body

bears...cruelty: has no sign in his face of great viciousness

youngest...nine: the last hatched and proverbially smallest of a
small bird's brood; a jest at Maria's size and, since the wren
flies rapidly, perhaps the speed of her entrance

the spleen: laughter (supposed to be governed by the spleen)

renegado: traitor to Christianity

such...grossness: such an impossibly ridiculous letter (and that
anyone could be so stupid)

pedant: inflexible, unimaginative schoolmaster

keeps a school i' th' church: runs a little village school (and is
thus provincial and unaware of the latest fashions)

dogged him: followed him at his heels

new map: a map of the East Indies, showing the coast of
Northern Australia for the first time, was published in 1599

SIR TOBY	We'll call thee at the cubiculo. Go.
	[Exit Sir Andrew
FABIAN	This is a dear manikin to you, Sir Toby.
SIR TOBY	I have been dear to him, lad – some two 50 thousand strong, or so.
FABIAN	We shall have a rare letter from him. But you'll not deliver't?
SIR TOBY	Never trust me then; and by all means stir on the youth to an answer. I think oxen and wainropes cannot hale them together. For Andrew, if he were opened and you find so much blood in his liver as will clog the foot of a flea, I'll eat the rest of th' anatomy.
FABIAN	And his opposite, the youth, bears in his visage 60 no great presage of cruelty.
	Enter MARIA
SIR TOBY	Look where the youngest wren of nine comes.
MARIA	If you desire the spleen, and will laugh yourselves into stitches, follow me. Yond gull Malvolio is turned heathen, a very renegado; for there is no Christian, that means to be saved by believing rightly, can ever believe such impossible passages of grossness. He's in yellow stockings.
SIR TOBY	And cross-gartered?
MARIA	Most villanously; like a pedant that keeps a 70 school i' th' church. I have dogged him like his murderer. He does obey every point of the letter that I dropped to betray him. He does smile his face into more lines than is in the new map with the augmentation of the Indies. You have not seen such a thing as 'tis. I can hardly forbear hurling things at him. I know my lady will strike him. If she do, he'll smile and take't for a great favour.
SIR TOBY	Come, bring us, bring us where he is.
	[Exeunt

Despite the danger, Antonio has followed Sebastian into
Illyria. He will not, however, go sight-seeing with
Sebastian since he was once in a naval battle against
Orsino's fleet and fears recognition.

---

make your pleasure...pains: take enjoyment from
  troublesome work

chide: criticize

filed: sharpened to a point like a spur (accent on '-ed')

And not all...unhospitable: it was not only my love of you,
  though I have enough of that to make me travel a greater
  distance, but concern that since you don't know this area
  you might have experienced difficulties here. This place has
  often been dangerous and inhospitable to unguided and
  friendless strangers.

shuffled...pay: inadequately rewarded with worthless money

worth...firm: wealth as great as is my knowledge of my debt
  to you

relics: ancient monuments

do renown this city: make this city famous

Count his: the common Elizabethan form of the possessive
  which would now be written 'Count's'

it...answered: I would hardly be able to defend myself in court

Scene 3

A Street
Enter SEBASTIAN *and* ANTONIO

SEBASTIAN   I would not by my will have troubled you,
             But since you make your pleasure of your pains,
             I will no further chide you.

ANTONIO   I could not stay behind you. My desire,
             More sharp than filed steel, did spur me forth;
             And not all love to see you – though so much
             As might have drawn one to a longer voyage –
             But jealousy what might befall your travel,
             Being skilless in these parts; which to a stranger,
             Unguided and unfriended, often prove   10
             Rough and unhospitable. My willing love,
             The rather by these arguments of fear,
             Set forth in your pursuit.

SEBASTIAN   My kind Antonio,
             I can no other answer make but thanks,
             And thanks, and ever thanks; and oft good turns
             Are shuffled off with such uncurrent pay;
             But were my worth as is my conscience firm,
             You should find better dealing. What's to do?
             Shall we go see the relics of this town?

ANTONIO   To-morrow, sir; best first go see your lodging.   20

SEBASTIAN   I am not weary, and 'tis long to night.
             I pray you let us satisfy our eyes
             With the memorials and the things of fame
             That do renown this city.

ANTONIO   Would you'd pardon me.
             I do not without danger walk these streets.
             Once in a sea-fight 'gainst the Count his galleys
             I did some service, of such note indeed,
             That were I ta'en here, it would scarce be answered.

Antonio says that the quarrel has still not been settled and proposes to go to their lodgings where Sebastian will rejoin him later. Antonio gives Sebastian his money in case he sees anything he wants to buy.

Belike: perhaps
Albeit the...time: although the circumstances of the time
for traffic's sake: for the sake of trade
lapsed: arrested
Elephant: a common inn sign – there was one in Southwark near the Globe Theatre
beguile the time: amuse yourself, disregarding time
toy: trifle, unnecessary thing
your store...markets: your wealth is not sufficient for anything other than necessities

SEBASTIAN	Belike you slew great number of his people?
ANTONIO	Th' offence is not of such a bloody nature, 30
	Albeit the quality of the time and quarrel
	Might well have given us bloody argument.
	It might have since been answered in repaying
	What we took from them, which, for traffic's sake,
	Most of our city did. Only myself stood out.
	For which, if I be lapsed in this place,
	I shall pay dear.
SEBASTIAN	Do not then walk too open.
ANTONIO	It doth not fit me. Hold, sir, here's my purse.
	In the south suburbs, at the Elephant,
	Is best to lodge. I will bespeak our diet, 40
	Whiles you beguile the time and feed your knowledge
	With viewing of the town; there shall you have me.
SEBASTIAN	Why I your purse?
ANTONIO	Haply your eye shall light upon some toy
	You have desire to purchase; and your store,
	I think, is not for idle markets, sir.
SEBASTIAN	I'll be your purse-bearer and leave you for
	An hour.
ANTONIO	To th' Elephant.
SEBASTIAN	I do remember.
	[Exeunt

Keeping track

Scene 1

1 When Feste says '*the Lady Olivia has no folly; she will keep no fool, sir, till she be married*' (Act 3 scene 1 lines 33–34) what does he mean?
2 What is Viola's assessment of Feste?
3 When Cesario addresses Olivia (Act 3 scene 1 line 85), what are Sir Andrew's reactions to her words?
4 How does Olivia feel about Cesario by the end of scene 1?

Scene 2

5 Why does Sir Andrew want to leave Olivia's house?
6 What opinions of Sir Andrew does Sir Toby give Fabian?

Scene 3

7 Why is Antonio fearful of remaining in Illyria? What, exactly, does he say he has done to offend Orsino?
8 What are Antonio and Sebastian's plans for their first day in the city? Where will they stay the night?

Discussion

1 In scene 1 Olivia commands that the garden gate be shut and Sir Toby, Sir Andrew and Maria leave. Apart from this being a practical action, it is also symbolic: it represents in a visual way what Olivia is thinking. Explain this.
2 At the beginning of scene 2 Sir Andrew is ready to leave but Sir Toby and Fabian wish him to stay.
    • Why is this?
    • How do they encourage Sir Andrew to stay?
3 In scene 3 Antonio is not keen to be seen on the streets of Illyria. Why is this and why is he so ready to give Sebastian his purse?

4 Why is the challenge which Sir Andrew sends to Cesario likely to have a comic outcome?

5 How many story-lines (plots) do you think the play now has? Briefly summarize what is happening in each plot.

Drama

Scene 1 lines 26–59

Work in pairs. Choose one of these sections: lines 26–37, 38–44, 44–51, 50–59

- Practise saying the words.
- What are the characters doing while they speak?
- Invent suitable moves and gestures.
- Show your piece to the rest of the class.

Scene 2 lines 38–48

Work in groups of three. Look at the way Sir Toby manipulates Sir Andrew. Divide up Sir Toby's lines between two people, for example:

   A: *Go, write it in a martial hand*

   B: *be curst and brief;* and so on.

- Work out the moves for the three characters. Remember, Sir Andrew is angry and ready for a fight. The other two are using the words like daggers. The fight has almost started already.
- Rehearse your performance and show it to the class.

Characters

Olivia

1 Olivia's behaviour changes as scene 1 develops. First she swallows her pride and tells Viola that a cypress hides her heart: in other words her feelings are only thinly veiled. Summarize her other changes of feeling and behaviour in this scene.

Viola

2 Viola has a difficult task in scene 1. Why? Point out the lines when she indicates that she is not what Olivia thinks she is.

Sir Andrew

3 In what ways does scene 2 prove Maria's statement that Sir Andrew is a great quarreller and an equally great coward?
   • What does the scene add to our understanding of the relationship between Sir Andrew and Sir Toby?
   • Sir Andrew claims that he would as much like to be a puritan as a schemer. Of which particular aspects of Sir Andrew's character would puritans disapprove?

Maria and Malvolio

4 Maria obviously derives great pleasure from making a fool of Malvolio.
   • Note specific phrases which show this in scene 2.
   • What is her assessment of his character?

Antonio and Sebastian

5 In what ways does the relationship between Antonio and Sebastian develop in scene 3?

Close study

Scene 1 lines 119–149

Use a photocopy of page 109.
• Read Viola and Olivia's conversation.
• Place the text in the centre of a larger piece of paper.
• Using colour, highlight lines which are spoken by one character directly to the other.
• Use different colours to highlight words which, you think, the speaker intended to keep to herself and the audience.
• On the left side of the larger piece of paper summarize Olivia's thoughts.
• Sum up Viola's thoughts on the right-hand side of the paper.
• Use arrows to indicate to which specific part of the text these thoughts apply.
• What themes, images or threads of thought gradually become evident in their words?

• Which of these do you think they would like to keep secret? From whom would they wish them to be kept secret?

Writing

1 Write the first draft of Sir Andrew's letter to Cesario. Follow Sir Toby's instructions in scene 2 lines 38–46.
   • Think about how Sir Andrew might begin, bearing in mind what we already know about his character.
   • It should contain some kind of reason for the challenge.
   • Might there be some things which he would not wish to include?
   • What might he exaggerate in the letter?
2 Imagine that Feste has decided to leave his job as jester. Olivia is advertising for a new one. Write the advert which is to appear in *Illyria Illustrated* and the complete job description which she sends out to applicants.

Quiz

Who:
   1 compares himself to a pilchard
   2 first speaks in French
   3 is a rare courtier
   4 is shut out
   5 has not given a heart to any woman
   6 will not stay a jot longer
   7 is to be found in his cubiculo
   8 is like a wren
   9 is like a murderer
   10 will order supper?

Olivia is planning to entertain Cesario. She calls for Malvolio because his seriousness suits her mood but is astonished by his new clothes and constant smiling.

---

bestow of: give to

youth...borrowed: Olivia refers to the proverb that 'it is better to buy than beg or borrow'

sad and civil: serious and dignified

possessed: by the devil, which was believed to be the explanation for some types of madness

tainted: diseased

as mad: i.e. possessed by Viola/Cesario

If sad...equal be: if my sad madness is equal to Malvolio's grinning lunacy

sonnet: love lyric; Malvolio then refers specifically to a ballad chorus in which it is asserted that all women want the same thing – to be in control

Scene 4

Olivia's Garden
Enter OLIVIA *and* MARIA

OLIVIA [*Aside*] I have sent after him; he says he'll come.
How shall I feast him? What bestow of him?
For youth is bought more oft than begged or
borrowed.
I speak too loud.
[*To Maria*] Where is Malvolio? He is sad and civil,
And suits well for a servant with my fortunes.
Where's Malvolio?

MARIA He's coming, madam; but in very strange manner.
He is sure possessed, madam.

OLIVIA Why, what's the matter? Does he rave? 10

MARIA No, madam, he does nothing but smile. Your
ladyship were best to have some guard about you if
he come; for sure the man is tainted in's wits.

OLIVIA Go call him hither. [*Exit Maria*] I am as mad as
he,
If sad and merry madness equal be.

Enter MARIA *with* MALVOLIO

How now, Malvolio?

MALVOLIO Sweet lady, ho, ho.

OLIVIA Smil'st thou? I sent for thee upon a sad occasion.

MALVOLIO Sad, lady! I could be sad. This does make some
obstruction in the blood, this cross-gartering; but 20
what of that? If it please the eye of one, it is with me
as the very true sonnet is, 'Please one and please all'.

OLIVIA Why, how dost thou, man? What is the matter with
thee?

Malvolio makes constant reference to the letter which, of course, entirely mystifies Olivia.

Not black in my mind: not melancholy (which was supposed to be caused by black bile)

the sweet Roman hand: the italic handwriting

go to bed: i.e. for a rest, to sleep off your madness

At your...daws: I will not answer you (Maria); melodious nightingales don't speak to the raucous jackdaws

made: a made man, i.e. rich, with a pun on mad

MALVOLIO	Not black in my mind, though yellow in my legs. It did come to his hands, and commands shall be executed. I think we do know the sweet Roman hand.
OLIVIA	Wilt thou go to bed, Malvolio?
MALVOLIO	To bed? Ay, sweet heart, and I'll come to thee. 30
OLIVIA	God comfort thee! Why dost thou smile so, and kiss thy hand so oft?
MARIA	How do you, Malvolio?
MALVOLIO	At your request? Yes, nightingales answer daws.
MARIA	Why appear you with this ridiculous boldness before my lady?
MALVOLIO	'Be not afraid of greatness.' 'Twas well writ.
OLIVIA	What meanest thou by that, Malvolio?
MALVOLIO	'Some are born great' –
OLIVIA	Ha? 40
MALVOLIO	'Some achieve greatness' –
OLIVIA	What sayest thou?
MALVOLIO	'And some have greatness thrust upon them.'
OLIVIA	Heaven restore thee!
MALVOLIO	'Remember who commended thy yellow stockings' –
OLIVIA	'Thy yellow stockings'?
MALVOLIO	'And wished to see thee cross-gartered.'
OLIVIA	'Cross-gartered'?
MALVOLIO	'Go to, thou art made, if thou desirest to be so' – 50
OLIVIA	Am I 'made'?
MALVOLIO	'If not, let me see thee a servant still.'
OLIVIA	Why, this is very midsummer madness.
	Enter SERVANT
SERVANT	Madam, the young gentleman of the Count

Cesario is announced and Olivia, assuming that Malvolio is ill, commands that he must be cared for. Malvolio continues to be convinced that his behaviour is exactly what Olivia wishes. Maria, Sir Toby and Fabian return, pretending to look after Malvolio.

---

entreat him back: persuade him to return

looked to: looked after

miscarry: harmed

dowry: marriage settlement, the wealth her husband would receive from her estate on her marriage

come near: understand

concurs directly: agrees precisely

a reverend carriage: a dignified way of carrying myself

the habit of...note: the clothes and manner of an important person

limed her: trapped her like a bird in sticky bird lime

fellow: social equal, but Malvolio misunderstands Olivia who uses the word in the more normal, patronizing manner of address to a servant

degree: social position

adheres: fits

dram, scruple: both very small weights, i.e. 'next to nothing'

no incredulous...circumstance: no unbelievable or uncertain event

full prospect...hopes: the complete fulfilment of my expectations

be drawn in little: were miniaturized, both in his body and in a portrait

Legion: the devil, referring to *Mark 5, 9* where Christ heals a madman who was possessed by a spirit of this name

	Orsino's is returned. I could hardly entreat him back. He attends your ladyship's pleasure.
OLIVIA	I'll come to him. [*Exit Servant*]. Good Maria, let this fellow be looked to. Where's my cousin Toby? Let some of my people have a special care of him; I would not have him miscarry for the half of my dowry.

60

[Exeunt Olivia and Maria, severally

MALVOLIO   O, ho, do you come near me now? No worse man than Sir Toby to look to me? This concurs directly with the letter: she sends him on purpose, that I may appear stubborn to him; for she incites me to that in the letter. 'Cast thy humble slough', says she. 'Be opposite with a kinsman, surly with servants; let thy tongue tang arguments of state; put thyself into the trick of singularity'; and consequently sets down the manner how; as, a sad face, a reverend   70
carriage, a slow tongue, in the habit of some sir of note, and so forth. I have limed her; but it is Jove's doing, and Jove make me thankful. And when she went away now, 'Let this fellow be looked to'. 'Fellow' not 'Malvolio', nor after my degree, but 'fellow'. Why, every thing adheres together, that no dram of a scruple, no scruple of a scruple, no obstacle, no incredulous or unsafe circumstance – What can be said? Nothing that can be can come between me and the full prospect of my hopes.   80
Well, Jove, not I, is the doer of this, and he is to be thanked.

Enter MARIA *with* SIR TOBY *and* FABIAN

SIR TOBY   Which way is he, in the name of sanctity? If all the devils of hell be drawn in little, and Legion himself possessed him, yet I'll speak to him.

FABIAN   Here he is, here he is. How is't with you, sir? How is't with you, man?

They pretend that they believe he is a lunatic, possessed by the devil.

---

discard: dismiss

private: privacy

how hollow...him: Malvolio is being '*surly with servants*' as the letter instructed him. Maria pretends that his unusual tone of voice is a sign of the devil which possesses him.

Carry...woman: take a sample of his urine to the woman who professes to be able to detect and combat witchcraft

Marry: surely. The word is a mild oath derived from the name of the Virgin Mary

move him: upset him

bawcock, chuck, Biddy: all are childish words of affection and all are variants on 'chicken'

'tis not...Satan: a dignified man should not play games with the Devil. Cherry-pit refers to a children's game, throwing cherry stones into a hole

foul collier: dirty coal miner; a reference to the devil and a play upon '*pit*'

MALVOLIO	Go off, I discard you. Let me enjoy my private. Go off.
MARIA	Lo, how hollow the fiend speaks within him. 90 Did not I tell you? Sir Toby, my lady prays you to have a care of him.
MALVOLIO	Ah ha, does she so?
SIR TOBY	Go to, go to. Peace, peace, we must deal gently with him. Let me alone. How do you, Malvolio? How is't with you? What, man, defy the devil; consider, he's an enemy to mankind.
MALVOLIO	Do you know what you say?
MARIA	La you, an you speak ill of the devil, how he takes it at heart. Pray God, he be not bewitched. 100
FABIAN	Carry his water to th' wise woman.
MARIA	Marry, and it shall be done tomorrow morning if I live. My lady would not lose him for more than I'll say.
MALVOLIO	How now, mistress?
MARIA	O Lord!
SIR TOBY	Prithee hold thy peace; this is not the way. Do you not see you move him? Let me alone with him.
FABIAN	No way but gentleness; gently, gently. The fiend is rough, and will not be roughly used. 110
SIR TOBY	Why, how now, my bawcock? How dost thou chuck?
MALVOLIO	Sir!
SIR TOBY	Ay, Biddy, come with me. What, man, 'tis not for gravity to play at cherry-pit with Satan. Hang him, foul collier!
MARIA	Get him to say his prayers, good Sir Toby, get him to pray.
MALVOLIO	My prayers, minx?
MARIA	No, I warrant you, he will not hear of godliness. 120

Malvolio, uncomprehending, storms off. The conspirators
decide that in order to continue the jest they will imprison
Malvolio – common treatment for the insane. Sir Andrew
returns with an absurd letter of challenge for Cesario.

---

of your element: I am not of your world, by which he means
social class but which, were he possessed by a devil, would
be literally true

His very genius...device: even his guardian angel has fallen for
the trick

take air...taint: become public knowledge and thus be spoiled

dark room and bound: a standard treatment for madness at
the time

penance: justified suffering

till our very...breath: until we are exhausted by our game

bring the device...bar: show the trick in open court so it may
be judged

More...morning: further fun and games fit for a holiday

scurvy: worthless, contemptible

nor admire...mind: don't be astonished

the blow of: the force of

MALVOLIO	Go, hang yourselves all! You are idle shallow things; I am not of your element. You shall know more hereafter. [*Exit*
SIR TOBY	Is't possible?
FABIAN	If this were played upon a stage now, I could condemn it as an improbable fiction.
SIR TOBY	His very genius hath taken the infection of the device, man.
MARIA	Nay, pursue him now, lest the device take air and taint. 130
FABIAN	Why, we shall make him mad indeed.
MARIA	The house will be the quieter.
SIR TOBY	Come, we'll have him in a dark room and bound. My niece is already in the belief that he's mad. We may carry it thus, for our pleasure and his penance, till our very pastime, tired out of breath, prompt us to have mercy on him; at which time we will bring the device to the bar and crown thee for a finder of madmen. But see, but see.

Enter SIR ANDREW

FABIAN	More matter for a May morning. 140
SIR ANDREW	Here's the challenge, read it. I warrant there's vinegar and pepper in 't.
FABIAN	Is't so saucy?
SIR ANDREW	Ay, is't, I warrant him. Do but read.
SIR TOBY	Give me. [*Reads*] 'Youth, whatsoever thou art, thou art but a scurvy fellow.'
FABIAN	Good and valiant.
SIR TOBY	[*Reads*] 'Wonder not, nor admire not in thy mind, why I do call thee so, for I will show thee no reason for't.' 150
FABIAN	A good note; that keeps you from the blow of the law.

Sir Andrew's ridiculous letter is read aloud and Maria tells him that Cesario is with Olivia. Sir Andrew is sent off to ambush him but Sir Toby keeps the letter since, as he tells the others, it will only prove to Cesario that Sir Andrew is an idiot and thus spoil the prospect of a fight. Sir Toby will instead deliver the challenge orally.

windy: down wind, like a ship sailing away from danger, or a hunter keeping clear of his quarry

bum-baily: bailiff, lying in wait to arrest a debtor

with a swaggering accent...off: spoken very confidently, loudly and belligerently

manhood more approbation: more evidence of manliness

let me alone: consider me the best

good capacity: sensible

clodpole: blockhead

set upon Aguecheek...valour: give Aguecheek a considerable reputation for courage

SIR TOBY   [*Reads*] 'Thou com'st to the Lady Olivia, and in my sight she uses thee kindly; but thou liest in thy throat; that is not the matter I challenge thee for.'

FABIAN   Very brief, and to exceeding good sense – less.

SIR TOBY   [*Reads*] 'I will waylay thee going home; where if it be thy chance to kill me' –

FABIAN   Good.

SIR TOBY   [*Reads*] 'Thou kill'st me like a rogue and a   160 villain.'

FABIAN   Still you keep o' th' windy side of the law. Good.

SIR TOBY   [*Reads*] 'Fare thee well, and God have mercy upon one of our souls! He may have mercy upon mine, but my hope is better, and so look to thyself. Thy friend, as thou usest him, and thy sworn enemy, ANDREW AGUECHEEK.' If this letter move him not, his legs cannot. I'll give't him.

MARIA   You may have very fit occasion for't; he is now in some commerce with my lady, and will by and   170 by depart.

SIR TOBY   Go, Sir Andrew; scout me for him at the corner of the orchard like a bum-baily. So soon as ever thou seest him, draw; and, as thou draw'st, swear horrible; for it comes to pass oft that a terrible oath, with a swaggering accent sharply twanged off, gives manhood more approbation than ever proof itself would have earned him. Away.

SIR ANDREW   Nay, let me alone for swearing.   [*Exit*

SIR TOBY   Now will not I deliver his letter; for the   180 behaviour of the young gentleman gives him out to be of good capacity and breeding; his employment between his lord and my niece confirms no less. Therefore this letter, being so excellently ignorant, will breed no terror in the youth; he will find it comes from a clodpole. But, sir, I will deliver his challenge by word of mouth; set upon Aguecheek a

Sir Toby hopes to convince Cesario that Sir Andrew is a dangerous adversary. Olivia gives Cesario a miniature picture of herself and invites him to return the following day. Sir Toby meets Cesario.

cockatrices: mythical serpents, basilisks, who killed an enemy by looking at it

give them way...after him: keep out of their way until Cesario goes and then immediately follow him

meditate the while upon: meanwhile I'll compose

laid mine honour...out: carelessly exposed my honour

reproves: blames

But such...reproof: but it is such a powerfully self-willed fault that it laughs at my attempt to control it

With the same...griefs: my master's grief causes him to behave in the same emotional way that you do

jewel: here a miniature portrait in a richly ornamental frame

it hath no...vex you: it can't nag at you

What shall...give?: You cannot ask for anything that I will refuse, providing I may give it without losing my honour.

acquit you: return it to you

A fiend like...hell: I would happily go to hell with a devil such as you

That defence thou...to't: prepare to defend yourself in whatever way you can

notable report of valour, and drive the gentleman –
as I know his youth will aptly receive it – into a
most hideous opinion of his rage, skill, fury and   190
impetuosity. This will so fright them both that they
will kill one another by the look, like cockatrices.

Enter OLIVIA *with* VIOLA *as* CESARIO

FABIAN   Here he comes with your niece; give them way till
he take leave, and presently after him.

SIR TOBY   I will meditate the while upon some horrid message
for a challenge.

                 [*Exeunt Sir Toby, Fabian, and Maria*

OLIVIA   I have said too much unto a heart of stone,
And laid mine honour too unchary out:
There's something in me that reproves my fault,
But such a headstrong potent fault it is   200
That it but mocks reproof.

VIOLA   With the same 'haviour that your passion bears
Goes on my master's griefs.

OLIVIA   Here, wear this jewel for me, 'tis my picture.
Refuse it not; it hath no tongue to vex you;
And I beseech you come again tomorrow.
What shall you ask of me that I'll deny,
That honour saved may upon asking give?

VIOLA   Nothing but this – your true love for my master.

OLIVIA   How with mine honour may I give him that   210
Which I have given to you?

VIOLA   I will acquit you.

OLIVIA   Well, come again tomorrow. Fare thee well.
A fiend like thee might bear my soul to hell.

                               [*Exit*

Enter SIR TOBY *and* FABIAN

SIR TOBY   Gentleman, God save thee.

VIOLA   And you, sir.

SIR TOBY   That defence thou hast, betake thee to't. Of what

Sir Toby warns Cesario that Sir Andrew is lying in wait for him. He says that Sir Andrew is a dangerous duellist and has killed three opponents. Cesario proposes to return to Olivia for protection but Sir Toby says that Sir Andrew has a legitimate quarrel and Cesario must fight him or lose his honour.

---

thy intercepter: the person that would ambush you

despite: indignation, anger

Dismount...yare: draw thy sword, be brisk

my remembrance is...any man: I can remember absolutely nothing which I have done to offend anyone

opposite: opponent

can furnish man withal: is able to arm a man with

dubbed...consideration: knighted at court, not on the battle-field. A cowardly, lazy soldier was described as a carpet-knight.

Souls and bodies...sepulchre: he has killed three men and he is now so angry that only by killing another can he be satisfied

Hob, nob: have or have not (life)

give't or take't: i.e. death

conduct: guard

taste: try out

belike: perhaps

very competent injury: sufficient insult

on, or strip your sword stark naked: go onwards (towards Sir Andrew) or unsheath your sword (to fight with me here and now)

meddle: fight

forswear...you: give up wearing a sword (and thus be dishonoured)

do me this courteous office: be kind enough

something of my...purpose: something I have failed to do rather than something I have done intentionally

nature the wrongs are thou hast done him, I know
not, but thy intercepter, full of despite, bloody as
the hunter, attends thee at the orchard-end.
Dismount thy tuck, be yare in thy preparation,   220
for thy assailant is quick, skilful, and deadly.

VIOLA   You mistake, sir, I am sure. No man hath any
             quarrel to me; my remembrance is very free and
             clear from any image of offence done to any man.

SIR TOBY   You'll find it otherwise, I assure you. Therefore, if
             you hold your life at any price, betake you to your
             guard, for your opposite hath in him what youth,
             strength, skill and wrath can furnish man withal.

VIOLA   I pray you, sir, what is he?

SIR TOBY   He is knight, dubbed with unhatched rapier   230
             and on carpet consideration, but he is a devil in
             private brawl. Souls and bodies hath he divorced
             three; and his incensement at this moment is so
             implacable, that satisfaction can be none but by
             pangs of death and sepulchre. Hob, nob, is his
             word; give't or take't.

VIOLA   I will return again into the house and desire some
             conduct of the lady. I am no fighter. I have heard of
             some kind of men that put quarrels purposely on
             others to taste their valour; belike this is a man   240
             of that quirk.

SIR TOBY   Sir, no. His indignation derives itself out of a very
             competent injury; therefore, get you on and give
             him his desire. Back you shall not to the house,
             unless you undertake that with me which with as
             much safety you might answer him. Therefore, on,
             or strip your sword stark naked; for meddle you
             must, that's certain, or forswear to wear iron about
             you.

VIOLA   This is as uncivil as strange. I beseech you do   250
             me this courteous office as to know of the knight
             what my offence to him is. It is something of my

Sir Toby goes to fetch Sir Andrew while Fabian keeps
guard over Cesario and further inflates Sir Andrew's
reputation. Sir Toby meets Sir Andrew and tells him that
Cesario is a tremendously skilful swordsman. Sir Andrew
says that he will give Cesario his horse if he will leave him
alone.

---

mortal arbitrement: fight to the death to resolve the issue
nothing of the circumstances more: (I know) nothing else
    about the situation
Nothing of that….valour: to look at his outward appearance
    you would not expect him to have the skill and bravery that
    you are likely to discover when you fight him
firago: virago, female warrior
pass, stuck in, the answer: all fencing strokes
with such a mortal…inevitable: with such a deadly
    movement that it is unavoidable
fencer to the Sophy: see Act 2 scene 5 line 175 and note
Pox on't: a mild oath referring to venereal disease; see the
    repetition in Sir Andrew's next speech as evidence of his
    limited command of language
an I: if I had
so cunning in fence: so skilled a swordsman
motion: suggestion

negligence, nothing of my purpose.

SIR TOBY   I will do so. Signor Fabian, stay you by this
gentleman till my return.   [*Exit*

VIOLA   Pray you, sir, do you know of this matter?

FABIAN   I know the knight is incensed against you, even
to a mortal arbitrement, but nothing of the
circumstance more.

VIOLA   I beseech you, what manner of man is he?   260

FABIAN   Nothing of that wonderful promise, to read him by
his form, as you are like to find him in the proof of
his valour. He is indeed, sir, the most skilful, bloody,
and fatal opposite that you could possibly have
found in any part of Illyria. Will you walk towards
him? I will make your peace with him if I can.

VIOLA   I shall be much bound to you for't. I am one that
had rather go with sir priest than sir knight. I care
not who knows so much of my mettle.
                                          [*Exeunt*

Enter SIR TOBY *with* SIR ANDREW

SIR TOBY   Why, man, he's a very devil; I have not seen   270
such a firago. I had a pass with him, rapier,
scabbard, and all, and he gives me the stuck in with
such a mortal motion, that it is inevitable; and on
the answer, he pays you as surely as your feet hit the
ground they step on. They say he has been fencer to
the Sophy.

SIR ANDREW Pox on't, I'll not meddle with him.

SIR TOBY   Ay, but he will not now be pacified; Fabian can
scarce hold him yonder.

SIR ANDREW Plague on't, an I thought he had been valiant   280
and so cunning in fence, I'd have seen him damned
ere I'd have challenged him. Let him let the matter
slip, and I'll give him my horse, grey Capilet.

SIR TOBY   I'll make the motion. Stand here, make a good

Sir Toby tells separately both Cesario and Sir Andrew that they must fight each other but that each will not hurt the other. As they reluctantly draw their swords Antonio enters and takes Cesario's side (believing him to be Sebastian). Both Antonio and Sir Toby draw their swords.

perdition of souls: loss of souls, death

I'll ride...ride you: Sir Toby puns on ride meaning, metaphorically, to manipulate, direct and dominate

take up: settle

as horribly conceited of him: imagining equally horrible things about him

he hath better...talking of: he has had second thoughts about his quarrel which he now finds to be hardly worth speaking of

for the supportance of his vow: merely in order to carry out his vow

the duello: duelling's strict code of conduct

I for him defy you: I will fight on his behalf

undertaker: one who undertakes someone else's business

show on't; this shall end without the perdition of
souls. [*Aside*] Marry, I'll ride your horse as well as I
ride you.

Enter FABIAN *and* VIOLA *as* CESARIO

[*To Fabian*] I have his horse to take up the quarrel.
I have persuaded him the youth's a devil.

FABIAN   He is as horribly conceited of him, and pants   290
              and looks pale, as if a bear were at his heels.

SIR TOBY   [*To Viola*] There's no remedy, sir, he will fight with
              you for's oath sake. Marry, he hath better
              bethought him of his quarrel, and he finds that now
              scarce to be worth talking of. Therefore draw for
              the supportance of his vow, he protests he will not
              hurt you.

VIOLA   [*Aside*] Pray God defend me. A little thing would
              make me tell them how much I lack of a man.

FABIAN   Give ground if you see him furious.   300

SIR TOBY   Come, Sir Andrew, there's no remedy; the
              gentleman will, for his honour's sake, have one bout
              with you – he cannot by the duello avoid it – but he
              has promised me, as he is a gentleman and a soldier,
              he will not hurt you. Come on; to't.

SIR ANDREW   Pray God he keep his oath.

VIOLA   I do assure you 'tis against my will.   [*They draw*

Enter ANTONIO

ANTONIO   Put up your sword. If this young gentleman
              Have done offence, I take the fault on me;
              If you offend him, I for him defy you.   310

SIR TOBY   You, sir? Why, what are you?

ANTONIO   One, sir, that for his love dares yet do more
              Than you have heard him brag to you he will.

SIR TOBY   Nay, if you be an undertaker, I am for you.

                                                    [*They draw*

Orsino's officers enter to arrest Antonio. He goes with them but asks Cesario for the money he had earlier given Sebastian. Cesario cannot understand his request but gives him half of the small amount of money he has on him.

I'll be with you anon: I'll be with you directly. It is not clear to whom Sir Toby is speaking. Is he sounding brave and addressing Antonio in the knowledge that the fight is about to be stopped or is he replying to Fabian, who may be trying to hide? Neither Fabian nor Sir Toby speaks again until Antonio and the officers have left.

that I promised you: i.e. the horse

do thy office: do your job

at the suit Of: because of a legal case against you made by

favour: face

my necessity: my need

It grieves me...myself: I am made more unhappy by the things which I will now be unable to do for you than by the troubles which affect me

lean...ability: very small amount of money

having: wealth

my present: that which I have with me at the moment

coffer: chest of valuables, here used ironically of her purse

Enter OFFICERS

FABIAN   O good Sir Toby, hold. Here come the officers.

SIR TOBY   I'll be with you anon.

VIOLA   [*To Sir Andrew*] Pray, sir, put your sword up, if you
            please.

SIR ANDREW Marry, will I, sir; and, for that I promised you
            I'll be as good as my word. He will bear you   320
            easily and reins, well. [*Sir Andrew and Viola put up
            their swords*]

1ST OFFICER This is the man; do thy office.

2ND OFFICER Antonio, I arrest thee at the suit
            Of Count Orsino.

ANTONIO   You do mistake me, sir.

1ST OFFICER No, sir, no jot; I know your favour well,
            Though now you have no sea-cap on your head.
            Take him away; he knows I know him well.

ANTONIO   I must obey. [*To Viola*] This comes with seeking
               you;
            But there's no remedy, I shall answer it.
            What will you do, now my necessity   330
            Makes me to ask you for my purse? It grieves me
            Much more for what I cannot do for you
            Than what befalls myself. You stand amazed,
            But be of comfort.

2ND OFFICER Come, sir, away.

ANTONIO   I must entreat of you some of that money.

VIOLA   What money, sir?
            For the fair kindness you have showed me here,
            And part being prompted by your present trouble,
            Out of my lean and low ability   340
            I'll lend you something. My having is not much;
            I'll make division of my present with you.
            Hold, there's half my coffer.

Antonio is deeply shocked when Cesario denies all
knowledge of him. He tells the officers that Cesario's
name is Sebastian and that he had saved him from a
shipwreck. After Antonio is taken away Viola recognizes
that this may be evidence of her brother's survival. Sir
Toby makes fun of Antonio's speech, which he has, of
course, found incomprehensible.

Is't possible...persuasion?: Surely you can be persuaded that I
  have deserved your help?

unsound: weak

Or any taint...blood: or any trace of the sins which we weak
  human beings may commit. (The metaphor suggests that
  vice is a disease which lives in our bodies.)

Relieved...devotion: in holy love I saved him and worshipped
  the goodness I saw in him

done good feature shame: shamed your appearance which is
  that of a good man. Antonio's speech here develops a theme
  which runs throughout this play (and generally in
  Shakespeare): how can we be sure that things really are what
  they appear to be? (See THEMES, page 224)

unkind: unnatural

empty...devil: handsome but soulless men are like empty
  coffers beautifully decorated on the outside

so do not I: I don't believe what I have just heard (that my
  brother is alive)

We'll whisper...saws: we'll recite some proverbs too; Toby
  mocks the mysterious conversation of Antonio and Viola
  which he and his friends have not understood

ANTONIO   Will you deny me now?
                     Is't possible that my deserts to you
                     Can lack persuasion? Do not tempt my misery,
                     Lest that it make me so unsound a man
                     As to upbraid you with those kindnesses
                     That I have done for you.

VIOLA   I know of none,
                     Nor know I you by voice or any feature.
                     I hate ingratitude more in a man   350
                     Than lying, vainness, babbling drunkenness,
                     Or any taint of vice whose strong corruption
                     Inhabits our frail blood.

ANTONIO   O heavens themselves!

2ND OFFICER   Come, sir, I pray you, go.

ANTONIO   Let me speak a little. This youth that you see here
                     I snatched one half out of the jaws of death,
                     Relieved him with such sanctity of love,
                     And to his image, which methought did promise
                     Most venerable worth, did I devotion.

1ST OFFICER   What's that to us? The time goes by; away.   360

ANTONIO   But O how vile an idol proves this god.
                     Thou hast, Sebastian, done good feature shame.
                     In nature there's no blemish but the mind;
                     None can be called deformed but the unkind.
                     Virtue is beauty, but the beauteous evil
                     Are empty trunks o'erflourished by the devil.

1ST OFFICER   The man grows mad. Away with him. Come,
                     come, sir.

ANTONIO   Lead me on.   [*Exit with Officers*

VIOLA   Methinks his words do from such passion fly,   370
                     That he believes himself; so do not I.
                     Prove true, imagination, O prove true,
                     That I, dear brother, be now ta'en for you.

SIR TOBY   Come hither, knight; come hither, Fabian. We'll
                     whisper o'er a couplet or two of most sage saws.

· **Viola exits, wrapped up in her hope of Sebastian's survival. The conspirators, seeing her behaviour to Antonio as a sign of Cesario's cowardice, encourage Sir Andrew to follow and hit him.**

I...glass: I see my brother when I look at myself in a mirror
fashion, colour, ornament: clothes of this colour, cut and decoration
paltry: worthless, contemptible
more a coward than a hare: Sir Toby alludes to the proverb that the hare is cowardly because it dares to pluck a dead lion by the beard
'Slid: by God's eyelid

ACTIVITIES

Keeping track

Scene 4

1 What reason has Maria for suggesting to Olivia that Malvolio is possessed by the devil?
2 What does Malvolio do and what does he say to Olivia which, he thinks, will show that he is responding to her love for him?
3 What do the conspirators do and say to Malvolio which is calculated to make him angry and confused?
4 Why does Sir Toby decide not to deliver Sir Andrew's letter to Cesario?
5 What is Sir Andrew like according to the description given to

VIOLA	He named Sebastian. I my brother know
	Yet living in my glass; even such and so
	In favour was my brother, and he went
	Still in this fashion, colour, ornament,
	For him I imitate. O, if it prove,
	Tempests are kind and salt waves fresh in love. [*Exit*

380

SIR TOBY	A very dishonest paltry boy, and more a coward
	than a hare: his dishonesty appears in leaving his
	friend here in necessity and denying him; and for his
	cowardship, ask Fabian.

| FABIAN | A coward, a most devout coward, religious in it. |

| SIR ANDREW | 'Slid, I'll after him again and beat him. |

| SIR TOBY | Do; cuff him soundly, but never draw thy sword. |

| SIR ANDREW | An I do not –   [*Exit* |

| FABIAN | Come, let's see the event.   390 |

| SIR TOBY | I dare lay any money 'twill be nothing yet. |

[*Exeunt*

Cesario by Sir Toby? How does he describe Cesario to Sir
Andrew?
6 Why does Antonio become involved in the duel?
7 What does Antonio ask Cesario to give him? What does
Cesario say in reply?
8 In what way has Antonio puzzled and excited Viola?

Discussion

1 This is one of the longest scenes in the play: divide it into
sections and summarize the action in each section in one short
sentence.
2 What parts of the scene do you find amusing, and why? In
how many different ways does Shakespeare create humour?

3 How does Olivia feel about Malvolio's behaviour? (Look especially at scene 4 lines 57–61.)

4 After Malvolio's humiliation in front of Olivia what do the others do to humiliate him further? Do you think they are fair to carry the joke so far?

5 Identify the taunts which Sir Toby uses to encourage Sir Andrew to fight. Explain how and why Sir Andrew changes his tune.

6 List examples of mistaken identity found in this scene

7 Fabian says: '*If this were played upon a stage now, I could condemn it as an improbable fiction.*'
   • Do you agree with his judgement?
   • What is amusing about his statement?

Drama

The letter

Work in groups of three or four. Read Sir Andrew's letter (scene 4 lines 145–168). Cast yourselves as Sir Andrew, Sir Toby, Fabian (and Maria if you are a group of four).
   • How does Sir Toby read the letter in order to extract maximum comedy from it?
   • How does Fabian interrupt and respond to the letter?
   • What are Sir Andrew and Maria doing while Sir Toby reads it?
   • Rehearse this exchange and perform it to the class.

The fight

The fight that doesn't happen is potentially very funny (scene 4 lines 284–307). Work in groups of six.
   • Imagine you are a team of fight coordinators brought in to choreograph this scene.
   • Cast the parts of Sir Andrew, Sir Toby, Cesario and Fabian.
   • The other group members direct the movements.
   • When you have worked them out, make drawings and diagrams to show the moves. You may need to invent a notation system to do this.

- When you have finished, swap your instructions with another group and see if you can recreate the scene from each other's notes.

Will you deny me now?

Antonio cannot believe that Sebastian will betray him (scene 4 lines 354–369). Work in groups of five or six.
- One person says Antonio's words, while the others become Viola, Antonio and the officers.
- The officers think the man has become mad. How do they behave?
- How angry does Antonio get?
- How does Viola respond? Remember she has already been involved in a fight with Sir Andrew.

Characters

Maria

1 Is Maria more vicious in her attitude towards Malvolio than anyone else? Look closely at the first 139 lines to find evidence that she doesn't want the humiliation of Malvolio to end.

Viola

2 Viola continues to show loyalty to Orsino in this scene. What other qualities does she exhibit? (Look at her scenes with Olivia, Sir Andrew and Antonio.)

Olivia

3 What mood is Olivia in at the beginning of the scene? Why does she call for Malvolio (line 5) and how does she react to his transformation?

Sir Toby

4 What evidence is there in this scene for the truth of the following statements about Sir Toby?
- He loves practical jokes.

- He really would like to turn Malvolio mad.
- He enjoys frightening people.
- He is no coward.

Malvolio

5 Describe Malvolio's behaviour from the points of view of (a) Olivia and (b) Sir Toby.

Close study

Lines 197–213

1 Olivia's lines show her to be more than a little unsettled.
- What does she say to Cesario?
- What does she actually want to say?
- Why is she unable to be more direct in her approach?

Lines 308–381

2 Create a simple cartoon to show the thought bubbles of Viola and Antonio. Is it likely that other characters might be aware of something having occurred? If so, include them and their thoughts in your cartoon.

or

On a copy of these lines highlight Antonio's accusations, pleadings and reasoning. Could he have said anything which would have cleared the situation at this point? How might the situation be resolved?

The whole scene

3 There are three kinds of writing in this scene: prose, blank verse and a type of rhymed verse known as heroic couplets (see pages 212 to 214).
- Read through the scene, noting where the changes between these three styles of writing occur.
- Look closely at lines 363–381. Why is rhymed verse used in this section?

Writing

1 *Illyria Illustrated* has recruited a Brownist (Puritan) newspaper columnist. S/he is visiting Illyria having been alerted to unsavoury behaviour said to have taken place there. The journalist wishes to find out whether the place is as wicked as it is made out to be. Write the feature article which the journalist produces following interviews with Malvolio and other characters at the end of Act 3 scene 4.

2 During the course of the scene Malvolio's emotions and thoughts change considerably. Write out his thoughts as a stream of consciousness – that is, as a continuous record of his private, internal speech. You might, for example, start: 'So Maria has come to fetch me at last! Are my garters neatly crossed? Then I'm ready. I hate these clothes, and having to smile... but I'll do anything to marry my lady. There she is now...'

3 Using Sir Toby's descriptions of Sir Andrew and Viola design a poster advertising their duel. You could adopt the style used by promoters of boxing and wrestling matches.

4 Antonio is taken to prison. Imagine he is put into a cell with another man accused of a similar crime. The other asks him, 'Why are you here and how were you caught?' Write Antonio's reply.

Quiz

Copy out the following paragraph, filling in the gaps. The answers are all names of characters.

Sir Andrew loves _____ but she loves _____, who loves _____, who loves _____. Antonio loves _____ who thinks that _____ is dead; she thinks that he is. Olivia thinks that _____ is mad but he thinks that _____ loves him. _____ thinks that lovers meet at the end of journeys, but perhaps he was only jesting!

Feste, sent by Olivia to find Cesario, comes across
Sebastian and asks him to go with him. Sebastian,
thinking the fool is jesting, gives him money to go away.
The conspirators enter, make the same mistake as Feste,
and Sir Andrew hits Sebastian.

1 Feste attempts to give Sebastian the message which Olivia   [1]
   had intended for Viola.

2 Feste laughs at Sebastian's use of the word '*vent*'.   [2]

3 Sebastian pays Feste to leave, threatening violence if he does   [3]
   not.

Act four

Scene

A Street
Enter SEBASTIAN *and* FESTE

FESTE   Will you make me believe that I am not sent for
you?

SEBASTIAN   Go to, go to, thou art a foolish fellow.
Let me be clear of thee.

FESTE   Well held out, i' faith. No, I do not know you; nor I
am not sent to you by my lady, to bid you come
speak with her; nor your name is not Master
Cesario; nor this is not my nose neither. Nothing
that is so, is so.

SEBASTIAN   I prithee vent thy folly somewhere else.   10
Thou know'st not me.

FESTE   Vent my folly! He has heard that word of some
great man and now applies it to a fool. Vent my
folly! I am afraid this great lubber, the world, will
prove a cockney. I prithee now, ungird thy
strangeness, and tell me what I shall vent to my
lady. Shall I vent to her that thou art coming?

SEBASTIAN   I prithee, foolish Greek, depart from me;
There's money for thee. If you tarry longer,
I shall give worse payment.   20

FESTE   By my troth, thou hast an open hand. These wise
men that give fools money get themselves a good
report, after fourteen years' purchase.

Enter SIR ANDREW, SIR TOBY, *and* FABIAN

SIR ANDREW   Now, sir, have I met you again? There's for you.
[*Strikes Sebastian*]

Sebastian beats Sir Andrew. Feste returns to Olivia to tell
her what has happened. Sebastian and Sir Toby draw their
swords and are about to fight when Olivia enters, angrily
dismisses Sir Toby and apologizes to Sebastian who she,
too, thinks is Cesario.

---

an action of battery against him: sue him for assault
put up your iron: sheathe your sword
you are well fleshed: you have already spilt enough blood
malapert: presumptuous, impudent
Fit for the...preached: fit to be savages who never had the
   opportunity to learn civilized behaviour
Rudesby: insolent, ill-mannered fellow
Let thy fair...sway: be ruled by reason not emotion
extent: violent attack

SEBASTIAN	[*Striking Sir Andrew*] Why, there's for thee, and there, and there.
	Are all the people mad?
SIR TOBY	Hold, sir, or I'll throw your dagger o'er the house.
FESTE	This will I tell my lady straight. I would not be in some of your coats for twopence. [*Exit* 30
SIR TOBY	Come on, sir; hold.
SIR ANDREW	Nay, let him alone: I'll go another way to work with him. I'll have an action of battery against him, if there be any law in Illyria. Though I struck him first, yet it's no matter for that.
SEBASTIAN	Let go thy hand.
SIR TOBY	Come, sir, I will not let you go. Come, my young soldier, put up your iron; you are well fleshed. Come on.
SEBASTIAN	I will be free from thee. What wouldst thou now? 40 If thou darest tempt me further, draw thy sword.
	[*Draws*
SIR TOBY	What, what? Nay, then I must have an ounce or two of this malapert blood from you. [*Draws*
	Enter OLIVIA
OLIVIA	Hold, Toby; on thy life I charge thee hold.
SIR TOBY	Madam!
OLIVIA	Will it be ever thus? Ungracious wretch,
	Fit for the mountains and the barbarous caves,
	Where manners ne'er were preached. Out of my sight!
	Be not offended, dear Cesario.
	Rudesby, be gone!
	[*Exeunt Sir Toby, Sir Andrew, and Fabian*
	I prithee, gentle friend, 50
	Let thy fair wisdom, not thy passion, sway
	In this uncivil and unjust extent

Sebastian, completely bemused, agrees to go home with
Olivia.

---

fruitless: pointless
Beshrew…me: damn him
started…thee: startled my heart, which I have given to you
What…this?: What pleasurable taste is this? What is meant?
How runs the stream?: Where are things leading? '*Stream*'
    perhaps suggested the reference to Lethe two lines later.
Or: either
Let fancy… steep: may love drown reason in the river of
    forgetfulness
Would thou'dst…me: I wish you to do as I command

Maria dresses Feste in the beard and gown of a priest, Sir
Topas.

Sir Topas: Sir was the customary title for a priest who had
    taken a university degree; topaz, a precious yellow stone,
    was believed to cure madness
the whilst: meanwhile
dissemble: disguise, be a hypocrite
to become…well: to fit the part. Perhaps Feste refers to the
    gown being too long or that he would not be tall enough to
    command a congregation from a pulpit.
to be said…scholar: to be called honest and hospitable is as
    good as being a painstaking scholar
competitors: allies, conspirators
Bonos dies: good day (corrupt Latin)
for as…but 'is'?: Feste pretends the tone and language of a
    pompous sermon

Against thy peace. Go with me to my house,
And hear thou there how many fruitless pranks
This ruffian hath botched up, that thou thereby
Mayst smile at this. Thou shalt not choose but go;
Do not deny. Beshrew his soul for me,
He started one poor heart of mine in thee.

SEBASTIAN What relish is in this? How runs the stream?
Or I am mad, or else this is a dream. 60
Let fancy still my sense in Lethe steep;
If it be thus to dream, still let me sleep.

OLIVIA Nay, come, I prithee. Would thou'dst be ruled by
me.

SEBASTIAN Madam, I will.

OLIVIA   O say so, and so be.

[*Exeunt*

Scene ❷ ────────────────────

Olivia's House
Enter MARIA *and* FESTE

MARIA Nay, I prithee put on this gown and this beard;
make him believe thou art Sir Topas the curate; do
it quickly. I'll call Sir Toby the whilst. [*Exit*

FESTE Well, I'll put it on, and I will dissemble myself in't;
and would I were the first that ever dissembled in
such a gown. I am not tall enough to become the
function well, nor lean enough to be thought a
good student; but to be said an honest man and a
good housekeeper goes as fairly as to say a careful
man and a great scholar. The competitors enter. 10

Enter SIR TOBY *and* MARIA

SIR TOBY Jove bless thee, master Parson.

FESTE Bonos dies, Sir Toby: for as the old hermit of

Feste, putting on an accent and a pompous form of speech appropriate to a priest, goes to visit Malvolio who is now imprisoned as a lunatic. Feste pretends that Malvolio's speech is entirely that of a devil which is possessing him. Malvolio complains of being in a dark cell but Feste claims that it is a light upper room.

Peace in this prison: Feste imitates a priest's greeting, 'Peace be in this house'.

counterfeits: plays the role

hyperbolical fiend: great devil. From this point until the exit of Sir Toby, Feste pretends to believe he is talking to a devil which possesses Malvolio. To delude Malvolio further he speaks in a contradictory and nonsensical manner.

How vexest thou: how you irritate and afflict

barricadoes: barricades, i.e. something impenetrable

clerestories: high windows

lustrous as ebony: as shining as deep blackness. These nonsensical paradoxes are designed to confuse Malvolio further.

Egyptians...fog: the plague of darkness, recounted in *Exodus 10, 22–23*

Prague, that never saw pen and ink, very wittily said
to a niece of King Gorboduc, 'That that is, is': so I,
being master Parson, am master Parson; for, what is
'that', but 'that'; and 'is', but 'is'?

SIR TOBY   To him, Sir Topas.

FESTE   What ho, I say. Peace in this prison.

SIR TOBY   The knave counterfeits well; a good knave.

MALVOLIO   [*Within*] Who calls there?   20

FESTE   Sir Topas the curate, who comes to visit Malvolio
the lunatic.

MALVOLIO   Sir Topas, Sir Topas, good Sir Topas, go to my lady.

FESTE   Out, hyperbolical fiend! How vexest thou this man.
Talkest thou nothing but of ladies?

SIR TOBY   Well said, Master Parson.

MALVOLIO   Sir Topas, never was man thus wronged. Good Sir
Topas, do not think I am mad; they have laid me
here in hideous darkness.

FESTE   Fie, thou dishonest Satan! I call thee by the   30
most modest terms, for I am one of those gentle
ones that will use the devil himself with courtesy.
Sayest thou that house is dark?

MALVOLIO   As hell, Sir Topas.

FESTE   Why, it hath bay windows transparent as
barricadoes, and the clerestories toward the south
north are as lustrous as ebony; and yet complainest
thou of obstruction?

MALVOLIO   I am not mad, Sir Topas; I say to you this house is
dark.   40

FESTE   Madman, thou errest. I say there is no darkness but
ignorance, in which thou art more puzzled than the
Egyptians in their fog.

MALVOLIO   I say this house is dark as ignorance, though
ignorance were as dark as hell; and I say, there was
never man thus abused. I am no more mad than

Feste claims that the reincarnation of human souls in
animal form is proper Christian belief. Malvolio refuses to
believe this heresy. Sir Toby calls a halt to Feste's jest and
says he wishes to find a way to end the trick on Malvolio.
Feste resumes his normal role and returns to Malvolio's
cell, singing.

---

constant question: organized test of reasoned argument
Pythagoras: an ancient Greek philosopher who believed that,
   at death, human souls might pass into animals
grandam: grandmother
haply: perhaps
allow of thy wits: believe you to be sane
woodcock: considered a foolish bird (see Act 2 scene 5 line
   79)
lest thou dispossess...grandam: in case you leave your
   grandmother's soul without a body to inhabit
I am for all waters: I can do anything
I would we...knavery: I wish we could conveniently escape
   from this practical joke
conveniently delivered: set free without causing us difficulty
I am now...upshot: Olivia is now so offended by my
   behaviour that I cannot see this joke through to the end
   without jeopardizing my position
[*Sings*]: and thus identifies himself to Malvolio
perdy: by God

	you are; make the trial of it in any constant question.
FESTE	What is the opinion of Pythagoras concerning wild fowl? 50
MALVOLIO	That the soul of our grandam might haply inhabit a bird.
FESTE	What thinkest thou of his opinion?
MALVOLIO	I think nobly of the soul, and no way approve his opinion.
FESTE	Fare thee well. Remain thou still in darkness. Thou shalt hold the opinion of Pythagoras ere I will allow of thy wits, and fear to kill a woodcock, lest thou dispossess the soul of thy grandam. Fare thee well.
MALVOLIO	Sir Topas, Sir Topas – 60
SIR TOBY	My most exquisite Sir Topas.
FESTE	Nay, I am for all waters.
MARIA	Thou mightst have done this without thy beard and gown; he sees thee not.
SIR TOBY	To him in thine own voice, and bring me word how thou find'st him. I would we were well rid of this knavery. If he may be conveniently delivered, I would he were; for I am now so far in offence with my niece that I cannot pursue with any safety this sport to the upshot. Come by and by to my 70 chamber.

[Exeunt Sir Toby and Maria

FESTE	[*Sings*] 'Hey, Robin, jolly Robin, Tell me how thy lady does.'
MALVOLIO	Fool!
FESTE	[*Sings*] 'My lady is unkind, perdy.'
MALVOLIO	Fool!
FESTE	[*Sings*] 'Alas, why is she so?'
MALVOLIO	Fool, I say!

Malvolio asks Feste to bring him writing materials.
Malvolio clings desperately to his sanity while Feste plays
the parts of both jester and priest.

how fell...wits?: how have you lost your reason?
so notoriously abused: so outrageously and publicly damaged
propertied me: treated me like a thing; ignored my humanity
face me out of: impudently tricked me out of
Endeavour thyself to sleep: try to sleep; the inclusion of the
   apparently redundant 'thyself' is to emphasize Sir Topas's
   belief that Malvolio is both himself and a body inhabited by
   the devil
shent: in disgrace
Well-a-day: alas

FESTE	[*Sings*] 'She loves another' – Who calls, ha?
MALVOLIO	Good fool, as ever thou wilt deserve well at my 80 hand, help me to a candle, and pen, ink, and paper. As I am a gentleman, I will live to be thankful to thee for't.
FESTE	Master Malvolio?
MALVOLIO	Ay, good fool.
FESTE	Alas, sir, how fell you besides your five wits?
MALVOLIO	Fool, there was never man so notoriously abused. I am as well in my wits, fool, as thou art.
FESTE	But as well? Then you are mad indeed, if you be no better in your wits than a fool. 90
MALVOLIO	They have here propertied me; keep me in darkness, send ministers to me, asses, and do all they can to face me out of my wits.
FESTE	Advise you what you say; the minister is here. [*As Sir Topas*] Malvolio, Malvolio, thy wits the heavens restore. Endeavour thyself to sleep, and leave thy vain bibble babble.
MALVOLIO	Sir Topas –
FESTE	Maintain no words with him, good fellow. [*As himself*] Who, I, sir? not I, sir. God be wi' you, 100 good Sir Topas. [*As Sir Topas*] Marry, amen. [*As himself*] I will, sir, I will.
MALVOLIO	Fool, fool, fool, I say –
FESTE	Alas, sir, be patient. What say you, sir? I am shent for speaking to you.
MALVOLIO	Good fool, help me to some light and some paper. I tell thee, I am as well in my wits as any man in Illyria.
FESTE	Well-a-day that you were, sir!
MALVOLIO	By this hand, I am. Good fool, some ink, paper 110 and light; and convey what I will set down to my

Feste, finally agreeing to bring Malvolio pen and paper, exits singing.

---

advantage thee more: do you more good
requite: repay
Vice: a character in morality plays, a type of fool, who
   sometimes carried a wooden dagger with which to fight and
   to cut the devil's nails

Sebastian is not sure whether he is really awake. Olivia has given him a pearl but he has lost Antonio.

'tis wonder...thus: I'm utterly amazed
was: had been
credit: reported opinion
though...madness: though both emotion and reason
   convince me that some mistake has been made rather than
   that I am mad

lady. It shall advantage thee more than ever the
bearing of letter did.

FESTE   I will help you to't. But tell me true, are you not
mad indeed, or do you but counterfeit?

MALVOLIO   Believe me, I am not. I tell thee true.

FESTE   Nay, I'll ne'er believe a madman till I see his brains.
I will fetch you light and paper and ink.

MALVOLIO   Fool, I'll requite it in the highest degree. I prithee
be gone.   120

FESTE   [*Sings*] I am gone, sir,
                    And anon, sir,
                 I'll be with you again,
                    In a trice,
                    Like to the old Vice,
                 Your need to sustain;
                 Who with dagger of lath,
                 In his rage and his wrath,
                    Cries, Ah ha, to the devil;
                 Like a mad lad,   130
                 Pare thy nails, dad.
                    Adieu, goodman devil.   [*Exit*

Scene ③

Olivia's Garden
Enter SEBASTIAN

SEBASTIAN   This is the air; that is the glorious sun;
            This pearl she gave me, I do feel't and see't.
            And though 'tis wonder that enwraps me thus,
            Yet 'tis not madness. Where's Antonio, then?
            I could not find him at the Elephant,
            Yet there he was; and there I found this credit,
            That he did range the town to seek me out.
            His counsel now might do me golden service;
            For though my soul disputes well with my sense

Though Sebastian cannot believe his senses he does not believe that either he or Olivia is mad. Olivia enters with a priest and he goes with them to a private chapel for a service of betrothal.

---

this accident...fortune: this unforeseen and great good fortune

all instance, all discourse: all previous experience and reasoned explanation

trust: trustworthy conclusion

sway: rule

Take and give...bearing: receive information, make decisions and give instructions with such a calm, discreet and stable manner

deceivable: deceptive

the chantry: the house's private chapel

Plight me...your faith: become formally betrothed; this was a legally binding contract committing the couple to get married at a later date

He shall conceal...my birth: the priest shall conceal our betrothal until you are willing for it to be made public, at which time we will be married in a manner appropriate to my social status

fairly note: look favourably upon

That this may be some error, but no madness,   10
Yet doth this accident and flood of fortune
So far exceed all instance, all discourse,
That I am ready to distrust mine eyes
And wrangle with my reason that persuades me
To any other trust but that I am mad,
Or else the lady's mad. Yet, if 'twere so,
She could not sway her house, command her
    followers,
Take and give back affairs and their dispatch
With such a smooth, discreet, and stable bearing
As I perceive she does. There's something in't   20
That is deceivable. But here the lady comes.

Enter OLIVIA *and* PRIEST

OLIVIA   Blame not this haste of mine. If you mean well,
Now go with me and with this holy man
Into the chantry by. There, before him,
And underneath that consecrated roof,
Plight me the full assurance of your faith,
That my most jealous and too doubtful soul
May live at peace. He shall conceal it
Whiles you are willing it shall come to note,
What time we will our celebration keep   30
According to my birth. What do you say?

SEBASTIAN   I'll follow this good man, and go with you;
And, having sworn truth, ever will be true.

OLIVIA   Then lead the way, good father; and heavens so
    shine
That they may fairly note this act of mine.

[*Exeunt*

ACTIVITIES

Keeping track

Scene 1

1 Sebastian is mistaken for his sister on three occasions. Who makes the mistakes and what are the consequences of each?

Scene 2

2 Feste is disguised in scene 2. As whom? Why?
3 What evidence is there in this scene that Malvolio is entirely sane?

Scene 3

4 What is Sebastian's state of mind at the beginning of scene 3?
5 To what does Sebastian agree at the end of the scene?

Discussion

1 Have Olivia's dreams come true?
   • Does she notice any change in her Cesario when she comes upon him in this Act?
   • What do you think her mistake indicates about her love for Cesario/Sebastian?
   • Is it relevant to remember that Olivia is mourning the death of her father and brother while Sebastian is also an orphan and believes his sister drowned?
2 Olivia has decided to keep her betrothal a secret. Why should she do this?
   • Does this fit in with the way in which we would expect her to behave?
   • What reasons does she give to Sebastian?
3 Has Malvolio been punished enough? Are you beginning to feel that those who are punishing him are going too far?
4 What different types of madness are mentioned in this Act?

- Do you think that anybody in the play is mad in the sense in which you would normally use the word?
- Is anyone mad in any other sense?

Drama

An alarming message

Work in pairs. Read again the first 30 lines of scene 1.
- Discuss what Feste reports to Olivia.
- Take the parts of Feste and Olivia and improvise the scene.
- Feste would probably act out the events in order to explain them better. How would Olivia react?
- When you have prepared your performance change partners with another pair so that Feste delivers his message to a different Olivia.

Unspeakable wrongs

Work in groups of three or four. One of your group is the outraged Malvolio. The others are lawyers. Malvolio asks the lawyers to prepare a case to right the unspeakable wrongs done to him.
- What advice can you give him?
- Remember he is paying you to help him.
- Who will he be bringing the case against?
- What questions would you wish to ask?

Characters

Sebastian

1 Consider all that we now know about Sebastian, including the things which we have heard him say and which others have said about him. Look at how he behaves towards Feste and Sir Andrew at the beginning of scene 1. What kind of a character is he? Can he be summed up in a few words? Is there any explanation for Viola and Olivia's strong feelings towards him?

Sir Toby

2 Why does Sir Toby stop Sebastian's fight with Sir Andrew? How does he react when Olivia tells him off? Is her summary of his character correct? (Look at scene 1 lines 46–50 and scene 2 lines 65–71.)

Malvolio

3 Remind yourself of Malvolio's description of Feste in Act 1 scene 5 lines 73–88. How does this affect the way Feste treats Malvolio in scene 2 of Act 4? Does Feste show any sympathy for Malvolio or willingness to help him out of his troubles?

4 When Malvolio thinks that he is talking to the priest, Sir Topas, how does he show that he is sane and intelligent? When he knows that he is talking to Feste does he show any humility? Do you think Malvolio's character is changing? Does he arouse sympathy in you?

Close study

Scene 2

1 List the ways in which Sir Toby and the others make a mockery of Malvolio in scene 2.
   • Is there anyone who appears to be taking the leading role?
   • Who is enjoying the prank most of all?
2 The unhappiness of Malvolio in scene 2 is reflected in the 'dark' thread which runs through the conversation which takes place.
   • Note all references to the theme of darkness.
   • Why does Shakespeare emphasize the image in this scene?
   • In what way is it symbolic of Malvolio's state of mind?

Scene 3

3 Sebastian is amazed at events. On a copy of scene 3, highlight the questions which he would like answered.
   • What are his concerns?
   • With what is he delighted?

- Which words show him willing to believe anything?
- Why, do you think, is he so ready to obey Olivia?

Writing

1 Malvolio obtains pen, paper and a source of light at the end of scene 2. Imagine that, as well as his letter, he writes a diary entry. What does he say about how he came to be in such a predicament? Whose fault does he believe it to be? What plans does he make for when he leaves his prison?

2 You are a journalist from *Illyria Illustrated* and you know all that has been going on. Stop and talk to Sebastian. Answer all his questions: explain what has happened and why he has been mistaken for someone else.

    Events in the play will now take an entirely different direction so write the story of what will happen, providing an appropriate ending for all the major characters. You could write the story in the style of a newspaper or magazine of your choice.

3 The priest who marries Olivia and Sebastian has known the family for years. When he gets home he tells another priest what has happened and how he feels about such a rapid change of behaviour and attitude in Olivia. He may have lots of wise and moral advice for other characters in the play. (Note that he is unlikely to see eye-to-eye with Malvolio: puritans did not accept the authority of priests.) Write the account he gives to his friend or, alternatively, draft his next sermon.

Quiz

Who says:
1 '*Are all the people mad?*'
2 '*Or I am mad, or else this is a dream*'
3 '*Do not think I am mad*'
4 '*Madman, thou errest.*'
5 '*I am no more mad than you are*'
6 '*And though 'tis wonder that enwraps me thus, Yet 'tis not madness.*'

Feste enters with Malvolio's letter from prison. He refuses to show it to Fabian. He meets Orsino with whom he bandies words.

his letter: i.e. Malvolio's letter

This...again: probably a topical allusion to Queen Elizabeth who was reported to have asked a member of her family, Dr Bullein, for his dog, in exchange for which she promised him anything he desired. When he had given the dog to her he duly asked her to return it to him.

her trappings: her trivial possessions

abused: deceived

conclusions...affirmatives: Feste, referring to the idea that two negatives make a positive, alludes to an argument in some Elizabethan love poetry in which the woman who twice says 'no' to a man who would like to kiss her is considered to have said 'yes'

By my troth: honestly

Act five

Scene

A Street
Enter FESTE *and* FABIAN

FABIAN   Now, as thou lovest me, let me see his letter.

FESTE   Good Master Fabian, grant me another request.

FABIAN   Any thing.

FESTE   Do not desire to see this letter.

FABIAN   This is to give a dog, and in recompense desire my
             dog again.

Enter DUKE, VIOLA *as* CESARIO, CURIO, *and* LORDS

DUKE   Belong you to the Lady Olivia, friends?

FESTE   Ay, sir, we are some of her trappings.

DUKE   I know thee well. How dost thou, my good fellow?

FESTE   Truly, sir, the better for my foes and the worse   10
             for my friends.

DUKE   Just the contrary: the better for thy friends.

FESTE   No, sir, the worse.

DUKE   How can that be?

FESTE   Marry, sir, they praise me and make an ass of me.
             Now my foes tell me plainly I am an ass; so that by
             my foes, sir, I profit in the knowledge of myself, and
             by my friends I am abused; so that, conclusions to
             be as kisses, if your four negatives make your two
             affirmatives, why then, the worse for my friends   20
             and the better for my foes.

DUKE   Why, this is excellent.

FESTE   By my troth, sir, no; though it please you to be one

Orsino pays Feste (who then begs for more) and sends him to tell Olivia of Orsino's arrival. Antonio enters under arrest but is recognized by Cesario as the man who rescued him from Sir Andrew. Orsino also recognizes him as an honourable enemy in battle.

---

double-dealing: giving twice, acting falsely

ill counsel: bad advice

Put...pocket: both, may Your Grace put his hand in his pocket to take out some money, and also, put your virtue away in order to give me money

Primo...tertio: first, second, third; probably a children's game of chance

triplex: triple time in music

tripping measure: rhythm for dancing

bells of Saint Bennet: obscure; possibly a reference to the bells of a church which stood close to the Globe Theatre or to a song now lost

bounty: generosity

covetousness: wanting to possess something which is not mine

Vulcan: the Roman god of fire and the patron of metalworkers

baubling: ridiculously small

For shallow...unprizable: not worth capturing because it was a small ship which could sail in shallow water

scathful grapple: harmful attack at close quarters

bottom: ship

very envy...loss: even his enemies, who were jealous of his success and had lost most

Cried fame...him: loudly praised him

of my friends.

DUKE   [*Giving a coin*] Thou shalt not be the worse for me
– there's gold.

FESTE   But that it would be double-dealing, sir, I would
you could make it another.

DUKE   O, you give me ill counsel.

FESTE   Put your grace in your pocket, sir, for this once,   30
and let your flesh and blood obey it.

DUKE   Well, I will be so much a sinner to be a double-
dealer: there's another. [*Giving a coin*]

FESTE   Primo, secundo, tertio, is a good play; and the old
saying is 'The third pays for all'. The triplex, sir, is a
good tripping measure; or the bells of Saint Bennet,
sir, may put you in mind – one, two, three.

DUKE   You can fool no more money out of me at this
throw. If you will let your lady know I am here to
speak with her, and bring her along with you, it   40
may awake my bounty further.

FESTE   Marry, sir, lullaby to your bounty till I come again. I
go sir; but I would not have you to think that my
desire of having is the sin of covetousness. But, as
you say, sir, let your bounty take a nap, I will awake
it anon.   [*Exit*

Enter ANTONIO *and* OFFICERS

VIOLA   Here comes the man, sir, that did rescue me.

DUKE   That face of his I do remember well;
Yet when I saw it last, it was besmeared
As black as Vulcan in the smoke of war.   50
A baubling vessel was he captain of,
For shallow draught and bulk unprizable,
With which such scathful grapple did he make
With the most noble bottom of our fleet,
That very envy and the tongue of loss
Cried fame and honour on him. What's the matter?

Antonio justifies himself and explains that he has been
defending, as he thinks, Sebastian. He cannot understand
why the young man refused to give him his money.

fraught from Candy: cargo (freight) from Crete
desperate...babble: regardless of his personal honour or public
  order, in a private brawl
put strange speech upon me: spoke strangely to me
but distraction: unless he were mad
Be pleased...off: allow me to discard
on base...enough: with sufficiently sound reasons
redeem: save
A wreck: lost at sea
without retention or restraint: without holding anything
  back or setting conditions
All his in dedication: I dedicated entirely to him
adverse: dangerous, full of potential adversaries
beset: set upon
Where being apprehended...acquaintance: at which point I
  was arrested and he, skilfully deserting me because he did
  not wish to share my plight, pretended not to know me
And grew a twenty...wink: in the twinkling of an eye he put
  the clock back twenty years (to a time before he was born)

1ST OFFICER	Orsino, this is that Antonio
	That took the Phoenix and her fraught from Candy;
	And this is he that did the Tiger board,
	When your young nephew Titus lost his leg. 60
	Here in the streets, desperate of shame and state,
	In private babble did we apprehend him.
VIOLA	He did me kindness, sir, drew on my side;
	But in conclusion put strange speech upon me.
	I know not what 'twas but distraction.
DUKE	Notable pirate, thou salt-water thief,
	What foolish boldness brought thee to their mercies,
	Whom thou, in terms so bloody and so dear,
	Hast made thine enemies?
ANTONIO	Orsino, noble sir,
	Be pleased that I shake off these names you give me: 70
	Antonio never yet was thief or pirate,
	Though I confess, on base and ground enough,
	Orsino's enemy. A witchcraft drew me hither.
	That most ingrateful boy there by your side,
	From the rude sea's enraged and foamy mouth
	Did I redeem. A wreck past hope he was.
	His life I gave him, and did thereto add
	My love without retention or restraint,
	All his in dedication. For his sake
	Did I expose myself, pure for his love, 80
	Into the danger of this adverse town;
	Drew to defend him when he was beset:
	Where being apprehended, his false cunning,
	Not meaning to partake with me in danger,
	Taught him to face me out of his acquaintance,
	And grew a twenty years' removed thing
	While one would wink; denied me mine own purse,
	Which I had recommended to his use
	Not half an hour before.

Orsino has just established that Antonio cannot be talking
about Cesario when Olivia arrives. She refuses to talk to
Orsino of his love and is surprised to see Cesario with the
Duke. Orsino accuses Olivia of ingratitude and
heartlessness.

No int'rim...vacancy: without pause, even for a minute
What would...serviceable: Olivia offers to serve Orsino in any
    way that is appropriate except that he may not have her love
    which is given to Sebastian/Cesario
Cesario: who Olivia sees standing close to Orsino
my duty hushes me: I cannot speak unless my lord commands
    it
If it be aught...tune: if it is the same as before
fat and fulsome: gross and sickly
To whose ingrate...tendered: to whom I have made a more
    faithful offer of love than any lover ever has but have been
    received ungratefully and with omens of failure. (Orsino
    uses the language of the traditional courtly lover to whom
    the lady is a goddess and her heart an altar where he must
    make sacrifice.)
Even what it...him: whatever it suits you to do and which is
    consistent with your noble status
th' Egyptian thief: who, in a popular Elizabethan translation
    of a Greek story, tried to kill the woman he loved so that she
    would be with him after his own death
sometime savours nobly: that once might have seemed like
    noble behaviour

VIOLA	How can this be?
DUKE	When came he to this town? 90
ANTONIO	Today, my lord; and for three months before, No int'rim, not a minute's vacancy, Both day and night did we keep company.

Enter OLIVIA *and* ATTENDANTS

DUKE	Here comes the Countess: now heaven walks on
	    earth.
	But for thee, fellow – fellow, thy words are
	    madness –
	Three months this youth hath tended upon me;
	But more of that anon. Take him aside.

OLIVIA	What would my lord, but that he may not have, Wherein Olivia may seem serviceable? Cesario, you do not keep promise with me. 100
VIOLA	Madam?
DUKE	Gracious Olivia –
OLIVIA	What do you say, Cesario? Good my lord –
VIOLA	My lord would speak; my duty hushes me.
OLIVIA	If it be aught to the old tune, my lord, It is as fat and fulsome to mine ear As howling after music.
DUKE	Still so cruel?
OLIVIA	Still so constant, lord.
DUKE	What, to perverseness? You uncivil lady, To whose ingrate and unauspicious altars 110 My soul the faithfull'st off'rings hath breathed out That e'er devotion tendered. What shall I do?
OLIVIA	Even what it please my lord, that shall become him.
DUKE	Why should I not, had I the heart to do it, Like to th' Egyptian thief at point of death, Kill what I love? – a savage jealousy That sometime savours nobly. But hear me this:

Orsino realizes that Olivia has fallen in love with Cesario
and threatens to tear out Cesario's eyes. Orsino prepares
to leave. Cesario says he will follow the man he loves and
Olivia accuses him of betrayal since they are now
contracted to be married. Cesario denies this. Orsino and
Olivia continue to argue over Cesario.

Since you...faith: since you ignore my love for you
And that: and because
screws: wrenches
minion: darling
I tender dearly: I offer to you only at a high price
that cruel eye: i.e. Olivia's, which, according to the
   conventions of love poetry, would reflect Cesario, the lover
   who has been '*crowned*' despite Orsino's anger
I'll sacrifice...dove: I'll kill you, Cesario, to spite the black
   heart of the fair Olivia
jocund, apt: cheerful, ready
To do you rest: to give you peace of mind
by all mores: by all similar comparisons
If I do feign...love: if I am not telling the truth heaven punish
   me for corrupting the love I feel
beguiled: deceived
it is...propriety: it is your fearful cowardice that makes you
   suppress your true identity
take thy fortunes up: accept what good fortune has given
   you, i.e. Olivia

Since you to non-regardance cast my faith,
And that I partly know the instrument
That screws me from my true place in your
   favour,   120
Live you the marble-breasted tyrant still.
But this your minion, whom I know you love,
And whom, by heaven I swear, I tender dearly,
Him will I tear out of that cruel eye
Where he sits crowned in his master's spite.
Come, boy, with me; my thoughts are ripe in
   mischief.
I'll sacrifice the lamb that I do love,
To spite a raven's heart within a dove.

VIOLA   And I, most jocund, apt, and willingly,
To do you rest, a thousand deaths would die.   130

OLIVIA   Where goes Cesario?

VIOLA   After him I love
More than I love these eyes, more than my life,
More, by all mores, than e'er I shall love wife.
If I do feign, you witnesses above
Punish my life for tainting of my love.

OLIVIA   Ay me detested, how am I beguiled!

VIOLA   Who does beguile you? Who does do you wrong?

OLIVIA   Hast thou forgot thyself? Is it so long?
Call forth the holy father.   [*Exit Attendant*

DUKE   [*To Viola*]   Come, away!

OLIVIA   Whither, my lord? Cesario, husband, stay.   140

DUKE   Husband?

OLIVIA   Ay, husband: can he that deny?

DUKE   Her husband, sirrah?

VIOLA   No, my lord, not I.

OLIVIA   Alas, it is the baseness of thy fear
That makes thee strangle thy propriety.
Fear not, Cesario, take thy fortunes up;
Be that thou know'st thou art, and then thou art

Olivia calls the priest as witness to their betrothal.
Emotions are running high as Sir Andrew enters to report
that someone has beaten himself and Sir Toby.

---

that thou fear'st: that of which you are afraid, i.e. the Duke
unfold: reveal
though lately…ripe: though we had previously intended to
  keep it secret the present events demand early revelations
passed: been agreed
contract: the priest uses legal language throughout this speech
  to emphasize the binding nature of the betrothal
mutual joinder: joining together
Attested: certified
holy close of lips: spoken vows, a kiss in church
in my function: in my presence, as priest
watch: clock, prayerful vigil
O thou…case?: You deceitful, sly fox cub! What will you be
  like by the time there are grey hairs in your fur?
craft: deceitful subtlety
thine own…overthrow: you'll trip yourself up
Hold…fear: keep some honour and honesty even though your
  behaviour frightens me
presently: immediately (in the present)
coxcomb: head; also refers to a fool's cap

As great as that thou fear'st.

Enter PRIEST

                    O, welcome, father!
Father, I charge thee, by thy reverence,
Here to unfold – though lately we intended
To keep in darkness what occasion now   150
Reveals before 'tis ripe – what thou dost know
Hath newly passed between this youth and me.

PRIEST   A contract of eternal bond of love,
Confirmed by mutual joinder of your hands,
Attested by the holy close of lips,
Strengthened by interchangement of your rings;
And all the ceremony of this compact
Sealed in my function, by my testimony;
Since when, my watch hath told me, toward my
     grave
I have travelled but two hours.   160

DUKE   [*To Viola*] O thou dissembling cub! What wilt thou
     be
When time hath sowed a grizzle on thy case?
Or will not else thy craft so quickly grow,
That thine own trip shall be thine overthrow?
Farewell, and take her; but direct thy feet
Where thou and I henceforth may never meet.

VIOLA   My lord, I do protest –

OLIVIA   O, do not swear!
Hold little faith, though thou hast too much fear.

Enter SIR ANDREW

SIR ANDREW For the love of God, a surgeon!
Send one presently to Sir Toby.   170

OLIVIA   What's the matter?

SIR ANDREW He has broke my head across, and has given Sir
Toby a bloody coxcomb too. For the love of God,
your help! I had rather than forty pound I were at

Sir Andrew accuses Cesario of causing the injuries. Sir Toby enters with a head injury. Feste, Fabian and the knights go to dress their wounds.

incardinate: incarnate, in the flesh (Sir Andrew characteristically gets the word wrong)

'Ods lifelings: by God's little life (more nonsense)

that that...on to do't: what I did I was persuaded to do

bespake you fair: spoke pleasantly to you

set nothing by: think nothing of

halting: limping

tickled...othergates: touched you with his sword in another way

That's all one: it's nothing

sot: fool, drunkard

agone: ago

set: closed, hidden like the sun when it has set

passy measures pavin: passemeasure pavan, a slow dance. Sir Toby compares the swaying dance step with the sleepy drunkard.

this havoc: Olivia refers both to their drunkenness and their injuries

dressed: bandaged

gull: dupe, fool; in this case Sir Andrew

home.

OLIVIA   Who has done this, Sir Andrew?

SIR ANDREW   The Count's gentleman, one Cesario. We took him
                  for a coward, but he's the very devil incardinate.

DUKE   My gentleman, Cesario?

SIR ANDREW   'Od's lifelings, here he is! [*To Viola*] You broke   180
                  my head for nothing; and that that I did, I was set
                  on to do't by Sir Toby.

VIOLA   Why do you speak to me? I never hurt you.
                  You drew your sword upon me without cause,
                  But I bespake you fair, and hurt you not.

                  Enter SIR TOBY *and* FESTE

SIR ANDREW   If a bloody coxcomb be a hurt, you have hurt me; I
                  think you set nothing by a bloody coxcomb. Here
                  comes Sir Toby halting; you shall hear more: but if
                  he had not been in drink, he would have tickled you
                  othergates than he did.   190

DUKE   How now, gentleman? How is't with you?

SIR TOBY   That's all one; he's hurt me, and there's the end
                  on't. [*To Feste*] Sot, didst see Dick surgeon, sot?

FESTE   O, he's drunk, Sir Toby, an hour agone; his eyes
                  were set at eight i' th' morning.

SIR TOBY   Then he's a rogue: and a passy measures pavin.
                  I hate a drunken rogue.

OLIVIA   Away with him. Who hath made this havoc with
                  them?

SIR ANDREW   I'll help you, Sir Toby, because we'll be dressed   200
                  together.

SIR TOBY   Will you help – an ass-head and a coxcomb and a
                  knave, a thin-faced knave, a gull?

OLIVIA   Get him to bed, and let his hurt be looked to.
                       [*Exeunt Feste, Fabian, Sir Toby, and Sir Andrew*

Sebastian enters, apologizing to Olivia for hurting Sir Toby. For the first time in the play the twins are together on stage. Everyone but Sebastian reacts to the situation: he apologizes to Antonio for losing him and only then sees Cesario. The twins begin to reveal their identities to each other.

the brother of my blood: my blood brother, my closest relative

I must...safety: I was forced to do it in order to preserve myself

You throw...me: you look at me oddly

so late ago: so recently

habit: dress, outward appearance

A natural perspective: an optical illusion devised by Nature

Nor can...everywhere: I am not a god, capable of being in two places at once

So went he suited: dressed exactly like you

spirits: ghosts

can assume both...suit: take on both appearance and dress (of the living person)

spirit: soul

that...participate: clothed on Earth in this rough body, which I have had since my birth

Enter SEBASTIAN

SEBASTIAN   I am sorry, madam, I have hurt your kinsman;
But, had it been the brother of my blood,
I must have done no less with wit and safety.
You throw a strange regard upon me, and by that
I do perceive it hath offended you.
Pardon me, sweet one, even for the vows   210
We made each other but so late ago.

DUKE   *confusion* —   One face, one voice, one habit, and two persons.
A natural perspective, that is and is not.

SEBASTIAN   Antonio, O my dear Antonio!
How have the hours racked and tortured me,
Since I have lost thee!

ANTONIO   Sebastian are you?

SEBASTIAN   Fear'st thou that, Antonio?

ANTONIO   How have you made division of yourself?
An apple, cleft in two, is not more twin
Than these two creatures. Which is Sebastian?   220

OLIVIA   Most wonderful.

SEBASTIAN   Do I stand there? I never had a brother;
Nor can there be that deity in my nature,
Of here and everywhere. I had a sister,
Whom the blind waves and surges have
    devoured.
Of charity, what kin are you to me?
What countryman? What name? What parentage?

VIOLA   Of Messaline; Sebastian was my father.
Such a Sebastian was my brother too;
So went he suited to his watery tomb.   230
If spirits can assume both form and suit
You come to fright us.

SEBASTIAN   A spirit I am indeed,
But am in that dimension grossly clad
Which from the womb I did participate,

Once Cesario is satisfied that Sebastian is who he says he is Viola reveals that she is his twin sister. Sebastian understands why Olivia behaved as she did towards him and Orsino begins to look on Viola/Cesario in a new light.

---

as...even: as everything else suggests that you should be
that record...soul: I remember it very well
lets: hinders
my masculine usurped attire: my inappropriate male clothes
cohere and jump: fit together and agree exactly
maiden weeds: woman's clothes
All the occurrence...fortune: all that has chanced to happen to me
But nature...that: but Nature ensured the right outcome (that Olivia is betrothed to a man, not a woman) even from an apparent mistake. The metaphor is from the game of bowls where the weighted bowl reaches its target by an indirect route.
contracted: betrothed
as yet...true: since the optical illusion in the perspective glass seems to be reality (see line 213)
over-swear: repeat with even greater emphasis
keep as true...night: I will keep my vows to you as faithfully as do the heavens which ensure that the sun rises and sets each day

	Were you a woman, as the rest goes even,
	I should my tears let fall upon your cheek,
	And say 'Thrice welcome, drowned Viola'.
VIOLA	My father had a mole upon his brow.
SEBASTIAN	And so had mine.
VIOLA	And died that day when Viola from her birth 240
	Had numbered thirteen years.
SEBASTIAN	O, that record is lively in my soul.
	He finished indeed his mortal act
	That day that made my sister thirteen years.
VIOLA	If nothing lets to make us happy both
	But this my masculine usurped attire,
	Do not embrace me till each circumstance
	Of place, time, fortune, do cohere and jump
	That I am Viola; which to confirm,
	I'll bring you to a captain in this town, 250
	Where lie my maiden weeds; by whose gentle help
	I was preserved to serve this noble Count.
	All the occurrence of my fortune since
	Hath been between this lady and this lord.
SEBASTIAN	[*To Olivia*] So comes it, lady, you have been
	mistook;
	But nature to her bias drew in that.
	You would have been contracted to a maid;
	Nor are you therein, by my life, deceived:
	You are betrothed both to a maid and man.
DUKE	Be not amazed. Right noble is his blood. 260
	If this be so, as yet the glass seems true,
	I shall have share in this most happy wreck.
	[*To Viola*] Boy, thou hast said to me a thousand
	times
	Thou never shouldst love woman like to me.
VIOLA	And all these sayings will I over-swear;
	And all those swearings keep as true in soul
	As doth that orbed continent the fire

Orsino wants to see Viola in her woman's clothes but discovers that the captain who helped Viola and has her clothes has been imprisoned by Malvolio. Feste appears with Malvolio's letter which he attempts to read as if a madman. Fabian is told to read the letter properly.

He upon...suit: he is in prison because of a lawsuit brought against him by Malvolio

enlarge him: set him free

much distract: mad

A most...banished his: my own passion caused me to forget his madness

he holds...end: he keeps the devil at a comfortable distance. The metaphor is from fighting with a quarterstaff.

case: situation

a madman's epistles are no gospels: a lunatic's letters are not to be read as true. Feste uses the biblical references here as a reminder that Malvolio's supposed madness is the result of possession by the devil.

it skills not much: it doesn't much matter

Look then...madman: Feste indicates that he is about to read the letter in a style appropriate for the mad Malvolio

Vox: voice (Latin)

perpend: consider, weigh up. The word is pompous, as is the rest of this sentence, and suggests Feste has resumed his impersonation of Malvolio or Sir Topas.

That severs day from night.

DUKE
                                    Give me thy hand,
And let me see thee in thy woman's weeds.

VIOLA
The captain that did bring me first on shore   270
Hath my maid's garments. He upon some action
Is now in durance, at Malvolio's suit,
A gentleman, and follower of my lady's.

OLIVIA
He shall enlarge him. Fetch Malvolio hither;
And yet, alas, now I remember me,
They say, poor gentleman, he's much distract.

Enter FESTE *with a letter, and* FABIAN

A most extracting frenzy of mine own
From my remembrance clearly banished his.
How does he, sirrah?

FESTE
Truly, madam, he holds Belzebub at the stave's   280
end as well as a man in his case may do. He's here
writ a letter to you. I should have given't you today
morning, but as a madman's epistles are no gospels,
so it skills not much when they are delivered.

OLIVIA
Open 't, and read it.

FESTE
Look then to be well edified when the fool delivers
the madman. [*Reads*] 'By the Lord, madam' –

OLIVIA
How now! Art thou mad?

FESTE
No, madam, I do but read madness. An your
ladyship will have it as it ought to be, you must   290
allow Vox.

OLIVIA
Prithee read i' thy right wits.

FESTE
So I do, madonna; but to read his right wits is to
read thus. Therefore perpend, my princess, and give
ear.

OLIVIA
[*To Fabian*] Read it you, sirrah.

FABIAN
[*Reads*] 'By the Lord, madam, you wrong me, and
the world shall know it. Though you have put me

It is obvious from the letter that Malvolio is not mad and Fabian is sent to release him. It becomes clear that Orsino will marry Viola. Olivia and the Duke agree on a double wedding. Malvolio is brought in.

I leave...injury: I forget my duty to you, the respect I ought to show, and speak directly from my sense of the injustice done to me

This savours...distraction: there is little suggestion of madness in this

these things: i.e. the revelations which preceded the entrance of Feste with the letter

think me...wife: consider me as a suitable sister-in-law, since you approved of me as a future wife

One day...on't: we will both marry, and thus create our alliance, on the same day

proper cost: own expense

I am most...offer: I am ready to accept your offer

So much against....sex: which was inappropriate for a woman

Notorious: undisguised and public

into darkness and given your drunken cousin rule
over me, yet have I the benefit of my senses as   300
well as your ladyship. I have your own letter that
induced me to the semblance I put on, with the
which I doubt not but to do myself much right or
you much shame. Think of me as you please. I leave
my duty a little unthought of, and speak out of my
injury.

THE MADLY-USED MALVOLIO.'

OLIVIA	Did he write this?
FESTE	Ay, madam.
DUKE	This savours not much of distraction.
OLIVIA	See him delivered, Fabian; bring him hither. 310

[Exit Fabian

My lord, so please you, these things further thought
   on,
To think me as well a sister as a wife,
One day shall crown th' alliance on't, so please you,
Here at my house and at my proper cost.

DUKE   Madam, I am most apt t' embrace your offer.
[*To Viola*] You master quits you; and for your
   service done him,
So much against the mettle of your sex,
So far beneath your soft and tender breeding,
And since you called me master for so long,
Here is my hand: you shall from this time be   320
Your master's mistress.

OLIVIA   A sister, you are she.

Enter FABIAN *with* MALVOLIO

DUKE   Is this the madman?

OLIVIA   Ay, my lord, this same.
How now, Malvolio?

MALVOLIO   Madam, you have done me wrong,
Notorious wrong.

Malvolio produces Maria's letter as explanation for his
behaviour. Olivia tells him that the letter has been written
by Maria and that he has been tricked. She promises him
that he can punish the tricksters. Fabian confesses that he
and Sir Toby are responsible.

from it: differently
not your invention: not devised and written by you
in the modesty of honour: as it befits a lady of your rank
such clear...favour: such apparent evidence of your good will
suffered: allowed
geck and gull: fool
That e'er invention played on: that ever was devised and
    practised
character: handwriting
now I do bethink me: now I remember
And in such forms...the letter: and in such clothes as the
    letter suggested for you
This practice...thee: this trick has wickedly passed judgement
    on you
plaintiff: prosecutor
Taint the condition: spoil the circumstances
I have wondered at: which I have been amazed by
Set this device: planned this trick
Upon some...him: because of his inflexible and rude
    behaviour to us

OLIVIA	Have I, Malvolio? No.
MALVOLIO	Lady, you have. Pray you peruse that letter.

MALVOLIO Lady, you have. Pray you peruse that letter.
You must not now deny it is your hand;
Write from it if you can, in hand or phrase;
Or say 'tis not your seal, not your invention;
You can say none of this. Well, grant it then,
And tell me, in the modesty of honour,   330
Why you have given me such clear lights of favour,
Bade me come smiling and cross-gartered to you,
To put on yellow stockings and to frown
Upon Sir Toby and the lighter people;
And, acting this in an obedient hope,
Why have you suffered me to be imprisoned,
Kept in a dark house, visited by the priest,
And made the most notorious geck and gull
That e'er invention played on? Tell me why.

OLIVIA Alas, Malvolio, this is not my writing,   340
Though, I confess, much like the character;
But out of question 'tis Maria's hand.
And now I do bethink me, it was she
First told me thou wast mad; then cam'st in
      smiling,
And in such forms which here were presupposed
Upon thee in the letter. Prithee be content,
This practice hath most shrewdly passed upon thee.
But when we know the grounds and authors
      of it,
Thou shalt be both the plaintiff and the judge
Of thine own cause.

FABIAN   Good madam, hear me speak,   350
And let no quarrel nor no brawl to come
Taint the condition of this present hour,
Which I have wondered at. In hope it shall not,
Most freely I confess myself and Toby
Set this device against Malvolio here,
Upon some stubborn and uncourteous parts

Fabian reveals that Sir Toby has married Maria. Only
Malvolio fails to see the funny side of the trick played
against him and swears to be revenged. Orsino looks
forward to his marriage with Viola. Feste is left alone on
the stage to sing.

---

importance: importuning, request

In recompense whereof: in payment for which

How with a sportful...sides passed: the practical joke was
without evil intention and should cause laughter rather than
revenge, once the grievances on both sides have been taken
into account

baffled thee: made you look ridiculous

interlude: short play

And thus...revenges: time, like Fortune's wheel or a spinning
top, changes the fate of each of us

convents: brings us together

A solemn...souls: i.e. we'll unite in marriage

habits: clothes

his fancy's queen: the sovereign of his heart, object of his love

A foolish...toy: (I was) a foolish child and not taken seriously

We had conceived against him. Maria writ
The letter at Sir Toby's great importance,
In recompense whereof he hath married her.
How with a sportful malice it was followed   360
May rather pluck on laughter than revenge,
If that the injuries be justly weighed
That have on both sides passed.

OLIVIA   Alas, poor fool, how have they baffled thee!

FESTE   Why, 'Some are born great, some achieve greatness,
and some have greatness thrown upon them.' I was
one, sir, in this interlude, one Sir Topas, sir; but
that's all one. 'By the Lord, fool, I am not mad.'
But do you remember? – 'Madam, why laugh you
at such a barren rascal? An you smile not he's   370
gagged'. And thus the whirligig of time brings in
his revenges.

MALVOLIO   I'll be revenged on the whole pack of you.   [Exit

OLIVIA   He hath been most notoriously abused.

DUKE   Pursue him, and entreat him to a peace;
He hath not told us of the captain yet.
                    [Exit Fabian or some other]
When that is known and golden time convents,
A solemn combination shall be made
Of our dear souls. Meantime, sweet sister,
We will not part from hence. Cesario, come –   380
For so you shall be, while you are a man –
But when in other habits you are seen,
Orsino's mistress and his fancy's queen.
                    [Exeunt all, except Feste

FESTE   [Sings] When that I was and a little tiny boy
        With hey, ho, the wind and the rain,
    A foolish thing was but a toy,
        For the rain it raineth every day.

    But when I came to man's estate,
        With hey, ho, the wind and the rain,

Feste's song describes the rather sad life of actors, jesters and human beings in general; despite which, he declares, he and his fellows will at least continue to try to make the audience laugh.

knaves and thieves: i.e. what I, as a clown, was thought to be
swaggering: bullying and showing off
With…heads: like all other drunkards I went to bed drunk

ACTIVITIES

Keeping track

1 Feste enters with a letter. Who has written it and to whom is it addressed?

2 What more do we learn about the reason for Orsino's grievance against Antonio?

3 What is Orsino about to discover from Antonio when he is distracted by Olivia's entrance?

4 Why does Orsino threaten to sacrifice Cesario?

5 What does Orsino find out just before the entry of the priest?

6 Why is Cesario surprised when Sir Andrew says to her, '*You broke my head for nothing*'?

7 Between line 205 and the end of the play what confusions and mistakes are finally sorted out? Are any situations left unresolved? Are there any characters who appear to end the play dissatisfied?

'Gainst knaves and thieves men shut their gate,   390
  For the rain it raineth every day.

But when I came, alas, to wive,
  With hey, ho, the wind and the rain,
By swaggering could I never thrive,
  For the rain it raineth every day.

But when I came unto my beds,
  With hey, ho, the wind and the rain,
With toss-pots still had drunken heads,
  For the rain it raineth every day.

A great while ago the world begun,   400
  With hey, ho, the wind and the rain,
But that's all one, our play is done,
  And we'll strive to please you every day.   [*Exit*

Discussion

1 What is the purpose of Orsino's conversation with Feste at the beginning of the scene?
2 Why was Orsino so surprised to see Antonio?
3 What are the other characters doing while Orsino and Antonio are speaking?
4 Why did Shakespeare set Fabian and Feste to read Malvolio's letter?
5 Is it appropriate to finish the play with a song? Is Feste's song the right one to use?
6 How has Malvolio '*been most notoriously abused*' and did he deserve it?

Drama

For the love of God, a surgeon!

- Work in groups of four.
- Read again lines 169–185
- Cast the parts of Sir Andrew, Olivia, Orsino and Viola and use FORUM THEATRE (see page 210) to explore the scene where Sir Andrew bursts in during the argument between Olivia, Orsino and Viola.
  - How do all the characters react?
  - Does the row continue through looks and glances, even though Sir Andrew demands most attention?
  - What is going through the minds of Olivia, Orsino and Viola?

The moment of revelation

Sebastian's appearance (lines 205–237) is the climax of the play. Work as a whole class group.

- Cast all the characters who are in the scene. The remainder of the group should be courtiers and officers.
- Create a still image of the moment, making sure that everyone is able to see and react to the situation. Sebastian must be entering the scene in such a way that he cannot initially see Viola.
- While someone reads the lines, slowly bring the scene to life.
- Do this several times trying out different reactions.
- Then read on further (to line 273) to see the other characters' spoken reactions.
- Who is last to speak? Why?
- Slow down the action so that you can listen to everyone's thoughts.
- This is a moment of wonder for the characters. How should it look to the audience?

Malvolio's letter

In groups of three cast yourselves as Olivia, Feste and Fabian and rehearse the reading of Malvolio's letter (lines 280–310). Extract the maximum humour from Feste's imitation of Malvolio and from the reaction of all three to Fabian's reading.

Characters

Olivia

1 How does Olivia feel when she hears Malvolio's letter? How does she react when she discovers that she has married Sebastian instead of Cesario/Viola?
   - List all the emotions which she experiences in this Act and beside them note the events which have caused her to feel them.

Viola

2 Why does Viola accept Orsino? He had said that he was only interested in Olivia. What happens to Viola during the Act and what emotional state is she in by the end?

Orsino

3 Why does Orsino so readily switch his attention from Olivia to Viola during this Act and accept Sebastian as a partner for Olivia?
   - What does this behaviour suggest about his character?
   - Is Shakespeare right in suggesting that people in love do behave in such an apparently irrational manner?

Sir Toby and Maria

4 We are told by Fabian (line 359) that Sir Toby has married Maria.
   - Have we been prepared for this event earlier in the play?
   - Can you find any moments when their affection for each other is shown?

Malvolio

5 When Malvolio is brought to Olivia by Fabian how does he speak to her?

- In what ways can we see that his relationship with her has changed?
- What does he accuse her of?
- Why does he become even more angry and storm out?
- What are the reactions of Olivia, Orsino, Feste and Fabian to him at the end?
- How do you feel about him now?

Who...?

6 Several of the characters are frustrated in this scene and the play ends with their problems unresolved. Who are they and what is the cause of their frustrations?

Close study

Lines 1–46

1 Explain how Feste obtains money from the Duke. What jokes and word-plays please Orsino?

Malvolio's defence

2 Read Malvolio's letter (lines 297–306) and his speech (lines 325–339):
- Put the letter into your own words.
- Describe the mood and tone of the letter (e.g. outraged, hurt, factual, sincere, pompous...).
- In what ways is the mood and tone of the speech different?

Review the whole act

3 In what order are the various plots of the play resolved?
- When you have listed them try to arrange them in a different order.
- Is Shakespeare's order the most dramatic or might it have been better, for example, to finish with Malvolio earlier in the scene or to make the twins meet each other later?

Writing

1 Write an alternative ending to the play, either as a dramatic scene or as a story.

- Where does Malvolio go when he leaves the scene?
- Does he hear Olivia's words?
- Would he come back at the Duke's bidding?

2 Write a one-act play or a short story called 'Malvolio's Revenge'. Use as many of Shakespeare's characters from *Twelfth Night* as you can.

3 Imagine that the puritan journalist on *Illyria Illustrated* arrives at the scene just in time to hear Antonio's speech. S/he decides to leave as Feste begins his song.
- Write his/her report of the events he has witnessed.
- S/he will be writing for the feature page and so you should make up suitable headlines and sub-headings.
- Remember that your style of writing will need to suit his/her character.

4 Imagine that you are the director of a production of this play. Using a series of diagrams and detailed notes show how the actors should move in the last act. Include all their entrances and exits and their positions on the stage. Think about these points:
- the shape of your stage
- where the audience is sitting
- where the entrances are
- what are the most dramatic moments? (Think especially about the entrances of Olivia, Andrew, Sebastian and Malvolio, and Malvolio's exit.)

Quiz

Exits and entrances

1 What does Feste enter with?
2 With whom does Cesario enter?
3 What two errands does Feste run?
4 Why does Olivia enter crossly?
5 Whom does Sebastian see first and whom last?
6 Who exits last?
7 Which major character apparently does not enter at all in Act 5?

Explorations

Keeping track

When you are studying a play one of the most difficult things to do is to keep track of all the ideas and information you gain as you work on it scene by scene. It is important to keep a note of what you do. Two good ways of organizing your work are to keep a SCENE LOG and a CHARACTER LOG.

Scene log

As you work on each scene, make a list of the basic information about it:
• when and where it takes place
• the characters in it
• what happens.
Then add any thoughts and comments you want to remember. You could use the layout illustrated opposite, or you may prefer to make up your own.

Character log

At the same time, you can keep a log for each of the main characters. Use this to record what you find out about the character in every scene he or she appears:
• key points about the character
• your reasons for choosing these
• the numbers of important lines
• short quotations to back up the key points.
Again there is a layout opposite, but you may prefer your own approach.

Scene log

Act/scene	Time/place	Characters	Action	Comments
1/1	Illyria: The Duke's Palace?	Orsino Curio Valentine musicians	Orsino is love-sick. Olivia, in mourning for her brother, will not see him or his servant.	Is Orsino in love with Olivia or with the idea of love?

Character log

Character: Orsino

Act/scene	Key points	Reasons	Key lines	Short quotations
1/1	He is in love.	Wants music to put him in the mood. Thinks Olivia cures illness.	1–2 20	'If music be the food of love, play on' 'she purged the air of pestilence'

Drama activities

Most of these activities can be done in small groups or by the class as a whole. They work by slowing down the action of the play and helping you focus on a small section of it, so that you can think more deeply about characters, plot and themes.

Hotseating

Hotseating means putting one of the characters 'under the microscope' at a particular point in the play. This is how it works:

1 Begin by choosing a particular character and a particular moment in the play. For example you might choose Malvolio, at the point where Olivia has commanded Maria and Sir Toby to look after him and his '*midsummer madness*' (Act 3 scene 4).

2 One person (student or teacher) is selected to be the chosen character.

3 That person sits 'in the hotseat', with the rest of the group arranged round in a semi-circle, or a circle.

4 The rest then ask questions about how the character feels, why s/he has acted in that way, and so on. Try to keep the questions going and not to give the person in the hotseat too much time to think.

Variations

1 The questioners themselves take on roles. (In the example above they could be the conspirators, the Duke's officers, or puritan friends of Malvolio.)

2 Characters can be hotseated at a series of key moments in a scene to see how their opinions and attitudes change.

3 The questioners can take different attitudes to the character, for example:
  - aggressive
  - pleading
  - disbelieving.

Freeze!

It is very useful to be able to 'stop the action' and concentrate on a single moment in the play. You can do this in a number of ways.

Photographs

Imagine that someone has taken a photograph of a particular moment, or that – as if it were a film or video – the action has been frozen. Once you have chosen the moment, you can work in a number of different ways:

1 Act that part of the scene and then 'Freeze!'. You will probably find it easier if you have a 'director' standing outside the scene to shout 'Freeze!'

2 Discuss what the photograph should look like and then arrange yourselves into the photograph.

3 One at a time place yourselves in the photograph; each person 'entering' it must take notice of what is there already.

4 Once you have arranged the photograph, take it in turns to come out of it and comment on it, with suggestions for improvements. There are a number of ways in which you can develop your photograph:

- Each person takes it in turn to speak his or her thoughts at that moment in the scene.
- The photograph is given a caption.
- Some members of the group do not take part in the photograph. Instead they provide a sound track of speech or sound effects, or both.

Statues/Paintings

Make a statue or a painting, like this:

1 Select a moment in the play, or a title from the play (e.g. '*My masters, are you mad?*'– Act 2 scene 3).

2 Choose one member of the group to be the sculptor/painter. That person then arranges the rest of the group, one at a time, to make the statue or painting.

Statues and paintings are different from photographs in two important ways:

- They are made up by an 'artist' and tell us about the artist's view of the person or event.
- If they talk, they tell us about what they can 'see', for example how people react when they see the statue or painting for the first time.

Forum theatre

In FORUM THEATRE, one or two people take on roles and the rest of the group are 'directors'. It works like this:

1 Select a moment in the play. (For example the moment when Olivia, accompanied by Maria, first sights Malvolio cross-gartered, in Act 3 scene 4 line 16.)
2 Select members of the group to be Olivia, Maria and Malvolio.
3 Organize your working area so that everyone knows where the other characters are, where characters make entrances and exits, and so on.
4 Begin by asking Olivia, Maria and Malvolio to offer their own first thoughts about position, gesture and movement.
5 The directors then experiment with different ways of presenting that moment. They can:
   - ask Olivia, Maria and Malvolio to take up particular positions, use particular gestures, move in certain ways
   - ask them to speak in a particular way
   - discuss with them how they might move or speak and why – for example to communicate a certain set of thoughts and feelings.
6 The short sequence can be repeated a number of times, until the directors have used up all their ideas about their interpretation.

Shakespeare's language

It is easy to look at the text of this play and say to yourself, 'I'm never going to understand that!'. But it is important not to be put off. Remember that there are two reasons which may make Shakespeare's language seem strange at first:
- He was writing four hundred years ago and the English language has changed over the centuries.
- He wrote mainly in verse. As a result he sometimes changed the order of words to make them fit the verse form, and he used a large number of 'tricks of the trade': figures of speech and other verse techniques (which are listed in the GLOSSARY, pages 235 and 236).

Language change

This can cause three main kinds of problem:

Grammar

Since the end of the sixteenth century, there have been changes in English grammar. Some examples:
- *Thee, thou, thy* and the verb forms that go with them have disappeared from Standard English. The Elizabethans made subtle distinctions between the pronoun *thou*, which they used familiarly or insultingly (rather like the modern French *tu*) and *you*, which was more formal.
  Consider the following words of Orsino in Act 5:
  '*…this your minion, whom I know you love…*'
  '*O thou dissembling cub!*'
  '*Give me thy hand*'
  What does *you, your, thou* and *thy* imply in each case?
- Words contract (shorten) in different ways. For example:
  'tis rather than *it's*
  who is't for *who is it.*
- Some of the 'little words' are different. For example: *an* for *if.*

Words that have changed their meaning

Sometimes you will come across words that you think you know, but discover that they don't mean what you expect them to mean.

For example: '*owe*' (Act 1 scene 5 line 307) means 'own' and '*antic*', which the Duke uses as an adjective meaning 'old-fashioned' (Act 2 scene 4 line 3), we would normally use as a noun describing inappropriate behaviour.

Words that have gone out of use

These are the most obvious and most frequent causes of difficulty. Shakespeare had – and used – a huge vocabulary. He loved using words, and pushing them to their limits. So you will come across many words you have not met before. They are usually explained in the notes.

The language of the play

Much of *Twelfth Night* is in blank verse but some sections are in various kinds of rhymed verse and parts are in prose.

Blank verse

The main part of the play is written in lines of ten syllables with a repeated pattern of weak and strong 'beats':

'*Conceal me what I am, and be my aid*'

(ti **tum** ti **tum** ti **tum** ti **tum** ti **tum**)

This pattern is called **iambic pentameter** (see GLOSSARY, page 235).

Had Shakespeare given every line exactly the same rhythm the play would soon become very monotonous so he varies the rhythm in a number of ways. Sometimes lines are not exactly ten syllables long or are divided between two or more characters. Often he just changes the pattern of weak and strong beats slightly:

'*Be not denied access, stand at her doors*'

(ti **tum** ti **tum tum** ti, **tum** ti ti **tum**)

He also expected the actors to speak his lines in a natural

manner, not pausing at the end of each line unless the sense of the words makes that necessary.

• Say the following lines twice, first pausing at the end of each line and the second time pausing only where there is a full stop:

'*A blank, my lord. She never told her love,*
But let concealment, like a worm i' the bud,
Feed on her damask cheek. She pined in thought,
And with a green and yellow melancholy
She sat like Patience on a monument,
Smiling at grief. Was not this love indeed?' (Act 2 scene 4 lines 111–116)

Your second reading should have made much more sense. Shakespeare uses the underlying rhythm to increase the compression and tension of Viola's words: it should assist and not get in the way of the expression of her emotion.

When the ten-syllable lines do not rhyme they are known as blank verse.

Rhymed verse

Sometimes Shakespeare uses a pattern of rhymed lines. It may be just two successive iambic pentameter lines, known as a heroic couplet:

'*Away before me to sweet beds of flowers:*
Love-thoughts lie rich when canopied with bowers.'

Such couplets are often used to round off a scene. They also increase emotional tension. Act 3 scene 1 ends with eighteen lines of heroic couplets and here, where both Olivia and Viola are trying to disguise their real emotions, the artificiality of the couplets helps to emphasize the unreality of the situation. *Twelfth Night* is especially notable for its number of songs: it begins and ends with music and Feste is given lyrics in a variety of metres.

Prose

Much of the play is written in prose – ordinary sentences – and it is not unusual to find a combination of prose, blank verse and rhymed verse in the same scene. Shakespeare chooses to use either verse or prose according to both the character and the situation.

- Look again at Act 5 and note who speaks in verse and who in prose.
- You will find that some characters use both verse and prose. Why do you think this is?
- Does it have anything to do with the people who are being spoken to or the types of conversation they are having?

The making of the play

'...we'll strive to please you every day.'

Shakespeare was an entertainer. He wrote plays and performed in them for the enjoyment of his audience. As Feste makes clear at the end of *Twelfth Night*, the audience must enjoy the play or they will not come back to the theatre for the next production. Shakespeare doesn't want the actors to starve.

Think of the plays, pantomimes and musicals that you have enjoyed seeing or the programmes that you make a point of watching on television. What ingredients have they had which interested you? Your list might include:

• humour
• suspense
• excitement
• violence
• music
• strong emotion
• entertaining characters.

Write down two examples from *Twelfth Night* for each of the ingredients in this list. If you have other ingredients which you think important to good entertainment can you find examples of them in *Twelfth Night*?

Such ingredients don't happen by accident. They have to be planned. Let's look at some of the ways in which Shakespeare builds the structure of the play.

Suspense

In Act 5 all the conflicts in the play reach a climax, relationships between the characters are sorted out and Sebastian and Viola re-discover each other.

• Make a list of all the conflicts and relationships which are resolved in Act 5.
• Are there any loose ends?

Take any one of the conflicts or relationships and chart its development through the whole play. For example, you could take the relationship between Viola and Sebastian, in which case your chart might start like this:

Act 1 scene 2: Viola believes Sebastian may have drowned though the Captain reassures her.

Act 1 scene 4: Three days later. No sign or mention of Sebastian.

Act 2 scene 1: Enter Sebastian…

Whichever conflict or relationship you charted you have probably noticed that it is not allowed to develop without interruption. Shakespeare switches between groups of characters. This enables him to increase our suspense while we wait to know what is going to happen.

Sometimes several days pass between one scene and the next. This is another reason why the play switches between groups of characters.

Plots and sub-plots

At the end of the play almost all the characters are on stage together. Until then they have largely been kept apart and the various plots have developed separately.

There are three main plot lines:
1 Orsino, Viola and Olivia
2 Sir Toby's Misrule: the manipulation of Malvolio and Sir Andrew
3 the wanderings of Sebastian.

• Which characters are involved in each of these plots? Copy the diagram on page 217 and complete it, placing crosses in the boxes as appropriate.
• There is one character who seems to be involved in all three plots from time to time. Who is he?

Shakespeare's plays often have a main plot and a sub-plot: that is, one story-line is more important than the other. Which is the most important plot in this play? Why? (Is there a right answer to that question?)

	Plot 1	Plot 2	Plot 3
Act 1 scene 1	X		
Act 1 scene 2			
Act 1 scene 3		X	
Act 1 scene 4			
Act 1 scene 5	X	X	
Act 2 scene 1		X	
Act 2 scene 2			
Act 2 scene 3			
Act 2 scene 4			
Act 2 scene 5			
Act 3 scene 1			
Act 3 scene 2			
Act 3 scene 3			
Act 3 scene 4			
Act 4 scene 1			
Act 4 scene 2			
Act 4 scene 3			
Act 5 scene 1	X	X	X

Humour

What types of humour do you find in *Twelfth Night*? To help you here is a list of some things which might make us laugh:
- jokes
- playing with words (**puns** – see GLOSSARY page 236)
- embarrassing situations
- pompous people

- mistaken identity
- secretly watching other people's silly behaviour.
1 Add to this list.
2 For each of the above briefly note an example from real life or the television and then find an example in *Twelfth Night*.

Dramatic irony

There is one special technique that Shakespeare uses both to make us laugh and to make us more involved in the action of the play.

Make a list of three occasions when:
1 we, the audience, know more about the situation in the play than the characters who are on the stage.
2 one character, or a group of characters, has a secret which is being kept from other characters who are on the stage at the same time

An example of (1) would be any scene after Act 1 scene 2 in which Viola appears as Cesario. An example of (2) would be in Act 2 scene 5 where Malvolio picks up the letter and says '*this is my Lady's hand*'.

You probably found many examples of this technique, which is called **dramatic irony**. It occurs throughout the play. In Act 5 the irony is especially rich since only the audience knows all the secrets of the various plots: the characters themselves have different levels of ignorance and confusion. The audience should be thoroughly involved in the play by this time and desperately eager to see how all the puzzles and frustrations will resolve themselves.

Themes

Shakespeare entertains us with a well-told story. He also asks us to think about, and react to, the experiences of his characters and the world they inhabit.

Their world may seem like a fantasy but the characters often behave very much like us.

If we examine some of the themes which run through the play we may have a clearer idea about Shakespeare's purpose, the ideas which he thought were important, and the ways in which his original audience, four hundred years ago, may have reacted to the play.

Love

Many of the characters in the play are in love.

- Write a list of the main characters. Against each name say who they love and give some evidence. (Don't forget that romantic love is not the only kind of love.) For example:
  Malvolio loves himself. '*O, you are sick of self-love, Malvolio*' (Act 1 scene 5 line 89).
  Love does not mean the same to each of the characters.

- Look again at Act 2 scene 4 and summarize what Orsino, Viola and Feste say about love.

Like many of Shakespeare's comedies *Twelfth Night* is a romantic play. It ends with three couples agreeing to marry. However, none of these marriages comes about in a very conventional manner.

- Write down the names of the three pairs of lovers at the end of the play and anything you know about their relationships which would suggest to you that they are entering into marriage for rather odd reasons.

The marriages seem to show that the world has been put right and all will live happily ever after. Yet most of the marriages in *Twelfth Night* seem less than ideal. Do one of the following:

1 For each couple describe what the next year or two of their married life is like. Would they continue to be happy? Would they argue? About what? What fault might they find with each

other? Who would be the more sympathetic and
understanding? (You could write your account as a story or
as a series of letters.)

2 Imagine that Shakespeare returned to the characters in
order to write a sequel. Write a summary of what happens
and a short scene from his proposed play.

Shakespeare understood the power which all kinds of love
exert over human beings. He also shows how dangerous and
deceptive love can be, especially to people who don't
understand themselves very well.

Self-deception

We have seen how secrets and deception are important to the
structure of the play. But *Twelfth Night* is also full of characters
who don't understand themselves. One sign of a lack of self-
knowledge is inconsistency when a person changes his or her
mind or is easily influenced by others.

• Review what you know about Orsino, Olivia and Malvolio.
In what ways is each of them inconsistent? Give examples of
two occasions when each changes his or her mind. What
does each of them not understand about themselves?

• Do you think that, by the end of the play, Orsino, Olivia
and Malvolio are any the wiser about themselves?

Other characters have varying degrees of self-awareness. Sir
Andrew, for example, is the least aware of any character. He
only has two moments of self-knowledge: at the end of Act 2
scene 3 and at the beginning of Act 3 scene 2.

• Look closely at the conversations he has with Sir Toby on
each occasion. What is Sir Toby able to do on each occasion
and what does this tell us about Sir Andrew?

It could be argued that the only character who has true self-
knowledge, and therefore understands most about the other
characters in the play, is Feste.

Misrule

There was a tradition in colleges, monasteries and the houses
of the nobility that Christmas fun and games were presided

over by a Lord of Misrule. The youngest, or the most lowly, person was given this role and placed in charge. Servants gave orders and their masters waited at table. Ridiculous punishments were awarded and practical jokes played. This tradition, sometimes called the Feast of Fools or the Feast of Asses, has almost entirely died out now but it can be traced back several centuries before Shakespeare and may have had its origin in the ancient Roman festival, the Saturnalia.

Feast of Fools

Twelfth Night is full of references to this tradition of the Feast of Fools and between them Feste and Sir Toby Belch are the Lords of Misrule. Here are some of the ingredients for a Feast of Fools. Find a quotation or incident in the play which is an example of each.

- Practical jokes.
- Violent and unjust punishment.
- The least able person being in charge.
- Servants telling their masters what to do.
- People wearing masks and other disguises.
- Fools being allowed to say what they like.
- Temporary chaos (order will be restored).

Shakespeare's audience would have recognized the references to the Feast of Fools in the play. The title and subtitle (*What You Will*) would also have given them a good idea of what to expect. They would have known that the Feast of Fools was a temporary thing and when Feste, at the end of the play, moves the play very firmly from fantasy to reality the audience would have known that all the characters return to the real world and some degree of good order, as well as to suffering: '*For the rain it raineth every day.*'

There is another way in which order has been removed, but it can never be restored. None of the young people has parents. Olivia is mourning the death of her father and Viola and Sebastian are also orphans. The Duke is apparently a young man without a father.

- How does this lack of parental control affect the way in which they all behave?

Madness

Another way of looking at the world of *Twelfth Night* is to see it as mentally disordered. Certainly several of the characters think that it is: 'mad' is a common word in the play.

- Find as many references to madness as you can. Write down brief quotations and who says them. Look particularly at Act 1 scene 5 lines 105–106, Act 2 scene 3 line 82, Act 3 scene 4 lines 14 and 53 and Act 4 scene 3 (Sebastian's first speech).
- Do you think that any of the people who are described as being mad really are insane? Are they mad in any other sense of that word?

'Mad' is a very imprecise word. (In fact, if you look the word up in a thesaurus you will find dozens of words with related meanings.)

- Write four sentences which each use the word 'mad' in a different sense.

  You could have used 'mad' to mean:
  - stupid
  - lacking caution
  - behaving riotously
  - deliberate fooling about
  - eccentric
  - in love
  - funny.

  Now apply each of your definitions of madness to a different character in *Twelfth Night*. Although none of the characters is mentally ill, most are, in some respects, mad.

Pleasure and puritanism; liberty and imprisonment

'*Dost thou think because thou art virtuous, there shall be no more cakes and ale?*'

At the heart of the play there is a conflict between freedom and confinement. During the course of the play many of the characters are either literally or metaphorically confined. For example, Antonio is literally locked up; Viola is metaphorically imprisoned in her disguise as Cesario.

• Find as many other examples as you can of characters who are either literally or metaphorically imprisoned.

Some characters, notably Feste and Sir Toby, demand freedom and refuse to be confined. In Act 1 scene 3 Maria tells Sir Toby: '*you must confine yourself within the modest limits of order*'. Sir Toby replies: '*Confine? I'll confine myself no finer than I am. These clothes are good enough to drink in, and so be these boots too…*'. He turns his answer into a joke about the state of his clothes but it is clear from this exchange that he has no interest in any kind of regulation of his behaviour.

• Can you find examples of the way in which Feste also pursues freedom and will not be tied down? Consider his first entrance in Act 1 scene 5, for example. Is there anything which restricts him?

Malvolio

Malvolio, on the other hand, is confined by his own code of behaviour and, towards the end of the play, literally imprisoned by Sir Toby. He loathes the freedom given to Feste, Sir Toby and their friends.

• What do you think Shakespeare's attitude is? Is he more sympathetic to Malvolio or to Sir Toby and Feste? At the end of the play is either side victorious?

When Shakespeare wrote *Twelfth Night* the puritans (see note on page 66) were gaining in political power and influence. They wanted the theatres closed because they saw them as distractions from humanity's true purpose: obedience to God and the pursuit of spiritual purity. Malvolio was a popular figure of fun from the earliest performances of the play.

The puritans, however, gained at least a temporary victory. In 1642, forty years after *Twelfth Night*, they came to power, rebelled against the king and closed the theatres. Plays were not performed again until 1660 when the monarchy was restored. Malvolio's threat to be revenged had been carried out.

Appearance and reality

Twelfth Night is a fantasy. In Illyria things are rarely quite what they seem to be.

- Which letters do not tell the truth?
- Who deliberately describes whom incorrectly, and to whom?
- Which characters are not what they seem to be?
- Who fails to understand another character's feelings towards him or her?

There are several possible answers to each of these questions. Illyria is a very confusing world to live in. But Shakespeare knew that it is often difficult to recognize the difference between truth and lies.

Throughout the play Shakespeare's audience would have been conscious of one kind of deception which we do not normally experience. This is because women did not act on the public stage in his time. Olivia and Maria would have been acted by young men, and the actor who played Viola would have been a man playing a woman who then had to act the part of a man, Cesario. This not only adds comic irony but constantly reminds the audience that things are not what they seem. Shakespeare often comments in his plays on the impossibility of knowing exactly what someone else is thinking or feeling.

- Look again at Viola's speech to the sea captain where she first comments about the difficulty of summing up someone else's character and then deliberately decides to disguise herself:

  '*There is a fair behaviour in thee, captain,*
  And though that nature with a beauteous wall
  Doth oft close in pollution, yet of thee
  I will believe thou hast a mind that suits
  With this thy fair and outward character.
  I prithee – and I'll pay thee bounteously –
  Conceal me what I am...' (Act 1 scene 2 lines 47–53)

  What, according to Viola in Act 5, has Malvolio done to the

sea captain? Does this tell us anything about Malvolio's ability to distinguish between appearance and reality? As events work out do you think it was a good idea for Viola to disguise herself?

Here are some further questions to think about though you may not wish to speak or write your answers!

- When was the last time you chose to disguise your feelings from someone else?
- When was the last time you thought someone was keeping their real thoughts or feelings from you?
- Would you always want to know what other people are thinking about you? Are there times when you would prefer not to know?

  'Now the melancholy god protect thee, and the tailor make thy doublet of changeable taffeta, for thy mind is very opal.'

Character activities

One of the most important things to do when studying a play is to get to know the characters really well. Keeping CHARACTER LOGS as you work through the play will give you plenty of raw material but it is also important to gain a picture of each character as a whole. The activities in this section will help you to do this.

Secret histories

In any play the writer presents us with key moments in the lives of the characters and leaves us to work out the rest of their biographies for ourselves. It is interesting to ask questions about those parts of the characters' lives that the writer does not tell us about. For example: where does Sir Andrew live and what is his life like when he is not visiting Sir Toby? What does Maria do when she is not scheming with Sir Toby and how did she happen to be working for Olivia?

1 Choose one of the main characters.
2 Make up a list of questions about that character that you would like to have answered.
3 Build up a complete 'secret file' about your chosen character. Start with his or her birth, family and childhood and add information up to the end of the play.
4 Use all the relevant information you can find in the play. You can make up as much as you like providing nothing contradicts the facts of the play and the behaviour of your character in it.
5 Include a section on the character's attitudes and ideas. Try to show the origins of any key relationships in the play.
6 If you wish, and if appropriate to the character, continue the character's existence beyond the time of the play. For example, you could report on the Duke and the success, or otherwise, of his marriage to Viola and his rule in Illyria.

Artist's brief

Characters in a play have to look right. Sometimes Shakespeare gives important clues about the appearance of his characters. When directors cast a production of a play they will think about the visual effect, and when we were designing this edition we had interesting discussions about how the characters should look. Eventually we gave the artist a detailed set of instructions which he then interpreted in the drawings which you have been looking at. Here is part of the artist's brief for this edition:

> *SIR TOBY BELCH A very fat drunkard – but not too tall, in order to contrast with his friend, Sir Andrew. He has expensive tastes but little money: a country squire and lay-about who loves all-night parties. Wears riding breeches and a hacking jacket. An irresponsible thirty-something. He once sang in the choir at school...*

- Choose three of the major characters and write your own artist's brief for each of them. Make sure that you use any instructions which Shakespeare gives for their appearance and dress.

Quotables

When you are talking or writing about a character it is important to be able to back up your ideas by referring to the play: 'This is true because in Act 1 scene 2 she says this or does that.' You should have plenty of this kind of information for the main characters in your CHARACTER LOGS.

You will need to keep some character information in your head and a good way of doing this is to search for 'the ideal quotation' for each character – the one line that absolutely sums up him or her. For example, Maria says of Malvolio: '*The devil a puritan that he is, or any thing constantly, but a time pleaser; an affectioned ass*'. Maria, of course, is biased against Malvolio but she does remind us here of several aspects of his character.

1 For each of the main characters find at least two short quotations. These may be something the character says or something another character says about him or her.

2 Select the best quotation from your list for each character.
3 Working in a group, try your quotations out on the others.
   Make a group list of the best quotation for each character.

Comparisons

Some characters can be easy to confuse with each other,
especially when they have important similarities. For example,
Sir Toby and Sir Andrew are both knights and are almost
always found together yet in many respects they have totally
different characters. Compare them with each other under
these headings:

Similarities	Differences
Knights	Sir Toby cheats and uses Sir Andrew
Fun-loving	Sir Toby is clever, Sir Andrew stupid
Hate Malvolio	Sir Toby is courageous, Sir Andrew a coward
Old friends	

(…and so on).
   When you have completed this table of comparison for the
two knights make a similar comparison for the following
couples:
• Viola and Sebastian
• Orsino and Olivia.

Writing about the play

Much of the writing you have been asked to do on the ACTIVITIES pages of this book has been personal or imaginative: telling the reader about your own response to an aspect of the play, or imagining that you were one of the characters in it. There is another kind of writing you will be asked to do, and that is writing about the play in a more formal way, for example: 'The play could easily turn into a tragedy. How are we made to feel that it will end happily?'

At first this kind of writing may seem rather daunting. It can certainly be difficult to prepare for and organize. The notes on these two pages are designed to help.

The question

What you must remember – first, last and all the time – is that you have been asked a particular question. You have not been asked to 'write all you know about *Twelfth Night*'. So at all stages of your work you must focus on the question. And there are two key questions you should ask yourself about it:
1 Am I sure that I understand what it means?
2 What is the best way to go about answering it?

Information and ideas

Before you can plan your writing in any detail, there are two things you need to do:

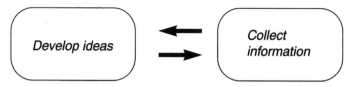

Each of these helps the other. Build up ideas by:
• talking to other people
• jotting down lists
• making a web diagram.

As you do so, you will begin to think of the information that you need. It is important to be able to back up each point you want to make by referring to something in the play: an action or a speech. You can use your SCENE and CHARACTER LOGS to help here. As you look at the logs and at the play itself you will begin to develop new ideas.

Making a plan

Some people can write well without making a plan, but this kind of more formal writing is difficult to do well without any plan at all. This is one way of planning:

1 Make a list of the main points you want to make.
2 Think of the best order to arrange these in. (Remember that someone is going to read what you write; you need to keep their interest, so don't, for example, use up all your good ideas at the beginning so that the second half of your writing is boring. Try to make sure that one point leads naturally to the next.)
3 Your last paragraph should state clearly your answer to the question, which you should have proved by everything else you have written.
4 Your first paragraph should introduce the topic – but don't give the game away at the very beginning!

The right tone of voice

If you are used to writing in personal and imaginative ways, you may find it difficult to get the right tone of voice for this kind of writing. As with other writing, it is important to think about the kind of person you are writing for.

Writing for exams

If it is an exam or test question, then you may well be writing for someone you have never met. So it may help you to imagine that your reader is a teacher from another school, someone who is not used to your way of writing and who does not know how you have been studying the play (and who does not necessarily share your sense of humour!)

Writing topics

Sometimes you may be asked to write a short response to a question or topic, while at other times you may be required to write at greater length. The topics on pages 231 to 234 give practice in both.

Short answers

Each of these topics requires detailed attention to a particular act, scene or part of a scene. The section referred to is stated at the beginning of each one.

1 **Act 1 scenes 1, 2 and 3**

In a very short period of time three groups of characters are introduced and three different moods established. What three contrasting moods do you find in these scenes? Use quotations to show how various kinds of verse and prose emphasize the differing moods.

2 **Act 1 scene 5**

In this scene Olivia finds herself at the centre of a series of conflicts between other people and within herself. What are the conflicts, what does Olivia do about them and what does the scene tell us about her?

3 **Act 2 scene 1 and Act 3 scene 3**

These scenes introduce us to Sebastian and Antonio. What do we learn about them and their relationship with each other?

4 **Act 2 scene 3**

Look closely at Maria's role in this scene. What do you observe about her relationship with both Sir Toby and Malvolio? Though she is physically small how does Shakespeare present her as a powerful woman?

5 **Act 2 scene 5**
   What different kinds of comedy do you find in this scene?
   Comment especially on the role of the hidden conspirators.
   (You may find it helpful to refer back to the section on
   HUMOUR on page 217.)

6 **Act 2 scene 3 and Act 3 scene 2**
   How does the relationship between Sir Toby and Sir
   Andrew develop in these scenes? In what ways does Toby
   manipulate Andrew?

7 **Act 3 scene 4**
   The action in this scene is fast and furious. What happens
   and in what ways have many of the major characters
   changed by the end of the scene?

8 **Act 4**
   Sebastian appears and is mistaken for Cesario. Who mistakes
   him and what are the consequences both for himself and for
   other characters?

9 **Act 5**
   All the confusions of the play are resolved but how far are
   the various characters satisfied by what happens? Do you
   think that justice is done for all of them?

Long answers

1 Feste has readily agreed to be part of the plot against Malvolio. How does he ensure that, at various times in the play, he keeps on the right side of his mistress? What does this tell us about him?

2 What do you think about Fabian and his role in the play? Is he an important character or could the play be performed without him?

3 If Shakespeare had not included the idea that Viola, Sebastian and Olivia were in mourning would the story have taken a different direction? Would you have expected the characters to have behaved differently? Would they have been under less emotional pressure and therefore been more rational?

4 'Olivia is firm but kind to her servants.'

Do you think that this judgement is true or does she fail to govern their behaviour properly? What evidence can you find in the play which reveals her relationships with them?

5 All of the following characters are selfish, spiteful or vain in one way or another: Orsino, Olivia, Feste, Sir Toby, Sir Andrew and Maria. Using what you have learnt about them throughout the play take two characters and defend them against the accusation.

6 Illyria could be described as a paradise for those who have few or no responsibilities, who can do whatever they please whenever they please. Do you agree or disagree with this point of view? Support your viewpoint with specific examples from the text.

7 A teacher is trying to decide whether or not to teach *Twelfth Night* to her class. Help her to make her decision by explaining your point of view.

8 'Malvolio is right to seek revenge at the end of the play. He is a good man who has been much abused.'

How far would you agree with this point of view?

9 Sir Toby may be funny and courageous but he is also a cheat and a liar. Do you think his behaviour can be justified? Should he be punished at the end of the play?

10 *Twelfth Night* is the story of a group of people who are on a journey of self-discovery. By the end of the play who has discovered what about himself or herself?

Glossary

Alliteration: A figure of speech in which a number of words close to each other in a piece of writing begin with the same sound:

'*I do I know not what, and fear to find*
Mine eye too great a flatterer for my mind.'

Alliteration helps to draw attention to these words and to the rhythm of the line.

Antithesis: A figure of speech in which the writer brings two opposite or contrasting ideas up against each other:

'*I would have men of such constancy put to sea, that their business might be everything and their intent everywhere; for that's it that makes a good voyage of nothing.*'

Apostrophe: A figure of speech in which a character speaks directly to a person who is not present or to a personification (see below):

'*O spirit of love, how quick and fresh art thou*
Jove, I thank thee. I will smile, I will do everything that thou wilt have me.'

Blank verse: See page 212

Dramatic irony: See page 218

Exeunt: A Latin word meaning 'They go away', used for the departure of characters from a scene.

Exit: A Latin word meaning 'He (or she) goes away', used for the departure of a character from a scene.

Hyperbole: Deliberate exaggeration, for dramatic effect. For example, when Sebastian is trying to impress Antonio with Viola's qualities he says:

'*she bore a mind that envy could not but call fair.*'

Iambic pentameter: A ten-syllable line of verse in which there are five *iambs*. An iamb is a pair of syllables stressed weak–strong (for example *today*).

Irony: When someone says one thing and means another. For example, when Sir Andrew says that he thinks life '*consists of eating and drinking*' Sir Toby replies, ironically, '*Thou'rt a scholar.*' This, like all Sir Toby's irony, goes over Sir

Andrew's head. See also Dramatic irony.

Metaphor: A figure of speech in which one person, or thing, or idea is described as if it were another:

'My desire,
More sharp than filed steel, did spur me forth.'

Onomatopoeia: Using words that are chosen because they mimic the sound of what is being described.

Oxymoron: A figure of speech in which the writer combines two ideas which are opposites. This frequently has a startling or unusual effect:

'I am slain by a fair cruel maid
Let me be boiled to death with melancholy'

(melancholy was supposedly cold).

Personification: Referring to a thing or an idea as if it were a person:

'She sat like Patience on a monument,
Smiling at grief.'

Play on words: see Pun.

Pun: A figure of speech in which the writer uses a word that has more than one meaning. Both meanings of the word are used to make a joke. For example, in Act 3 scene 1 lines 1–3, *'live'* is used by Viola to mean 'earn a living' and by Feste to mean 'lodge'. At the beginning of Act 1 scene 5 Maria and Feste have a punning competition where they play with the words *'hang'*, *'colours'* and *'points'*.

Simile: A comparison between two things which the writer makes clear by using words such as 'like' or 'as':

'I'd beat him like a dog'

Soliloquy: When a character is alone on stage, or separated from the other characters in some way and speaks apparently to himself or herself. For example, Sebastian at the beginning of Act 4 scene 3.